# 101
## GREAT OUTDOOR GETAWAYS

# 101
## GREAT OUTDOOR GETAWAYS

**Bounty**
Books

**Publisher:** Polly Manguel
**Project Editor:** Emma Hill
**Designer:** Ron Callow/Design 23
**Production Manager:** Neil Randles

This edition first published in Great Britain in 2012 by
Bounty Books, a division of Octopus Publishing Group Limited
Endeavour House,
189 Shaftesbury Avenue,
London WC2H 8JY
www.octopusbooks.co.uk

An Hachette UK Company
www.hachette.co.uk

Text previously appeared in:
*501 Must-Visit Destinations*
*501 Must-Visit Natural Wonders*
*501 Must-Visit Islands*
*501 Must-Take Journeys*
*501 Must-Visit Wild Places*

A CIP catalogue record is available from the British Library

ISBN: 978-0-753723-07-4

Printed and bound in China

**Please note:**
We now know that political situations arise very quickly and a city or country that
was quite safe a short time ago can suddenly become a 'no-go' area. Please
check with the relevant authorities before booking tickets and travelling if you
think there could be a problem.

The seasons given in this book relate to the relevant hemisphere. Be sure to
check that you visit at the correct time.

# Contents

# Introduction

Planet Earth is having a hard time coping with population explosion, rapid industrialization and global pollution that threatens the very future of humankind. Most people in the developed world have to live in sprawling cities, and many find the everyday strain of doing so gets harder to bear with every passing year. Sometimes, when contemplating endless queues for this and that, streets clogged with fume-belching traffic, overcrowded commuter trains and the stresses of modern urban life, it's tempting to assume that our unremitting quest for advancement is demanding too high a price in terms of lifestyle quality. And awareness of the damage we're inflicting on an environment that sustains us all is equally alarming, belatedly forcing politicians everywhere to start talking about (and sometimes even introducing) green policies aimed at mitigating increasing pollution and degradation of the world's natural resources, before it's too late.

Faced with those alarming negatives, it's sometimes far too easy to overlook the greatest positive of all. Despite our worst efforts to spoil and degrade it, the natural world remains a truly magical place. From pristine islands set in azure seas to snow-capped mountains, dense rain forests to wide African plains, untamed wilderness to treasured national parks, glaciers to volcanoes, the sheer splendour of nature in its many forms can and does retain the power to surprise and delight us. This book highlights some of the very best places that

underline that message – places so special they lift our souls even as they remind us of what we're in danger of losing. But forget that for a moment, and simply enjoy reading about some of the world's most stunning locations. Better still, start planning great outdoor getaways that will let you see and fully appreciate some of these breathtaking wonders for yourself.

And by going in search of stunning scenery and exciting wildlife, adventurous travellers who look for so much more than packaged beach holidays can help preserve the very things they take the trouble to find, for eco-tourism is a powerful force in protecting and sustaining fragile habitats and endangered wildlife which would otherwise be threatened. By generating revenue for countries and local communities in desperate need of resources, visitors can encourage sustainable development that avoids degradation and helps protect the planet's precious – and shrinking – natural jewels. By even reading and talking about the sort of inspiring places described on these pages, you will encourage growing awareness that they must be protected before it's too late. By actually visiting some of them you can contribute to their continued preservation, so generations yet to come can experience the same excitement and sense of awe at nature's commanding majesty. Will all the dramatic sights in this book – and others like them – still be unspoiled in a century's time? Nobody can answer that question, but one thing's for sure: they're out there now, so we lucky ones may still appreciate and enjoy them – in our minds or in person.

# AFRICA

# Waza National Park

Waza National Park is a vast, remote area in the far North Province of Cameroon. Situated on the edge of the Sahel, between Chad and Nigeria, these flat acacia plains lie to the south of Lake Chad's floodplain, and are only accessible from mid-November to mid-June due to summertime flooding.

The park, which is an area of about 170,000 hectares (420,000 acres), was listed as a UNESCO Biosphere Reserve in 1982. It consists of a forested area, and huge expanses of feathery grasslands and seasonal marshes, making it home both to forest and savannah animals, as well as permanent and migrating birds.

This is probably the best place in Central Africa to observe wildlife, and in late spring, when only a few waterholes remain, a constant parade of fabulous animals arrive in search of water and shade, finding moments of much needed relief from the blistering sun.

The plains are teeming with animals – giraffe, antelope, hyena, cheetah, serval, warthog, elephants and lions. A multitude of birds can be seen here, as both African and Palearctic migrants are attracted by the habitat. Some 397 species have been sighted, including raptors such as griffon vultures, eagles, goshawks and buzzards, flocks of cranes, storks and egrets, and many species of migrant ducks and waders.

Needless to say, Waza National Park suffers from poaching. Unfortunately there are very few guards, making it impossible to secure the entire area, even with extra funding given by the World Wildlife Fund and the Netherlands IUCN Committee. Visit as part of an organized tour or bring your own 4 wheel drive vehicle. Whatever way you travel, you are bound to see a wealth of marvellous creatures roaming these golden plains.

**WHAT IS IT?**
A vast area of plains and woods, where a myriad of birds and animals can be observed.
**HOW TO GET THERE:**
By 4 wheel drive from Maroua.
**WHEN TO GO:**
Mid-November to mid-June, but April/May is the optimum time to see lions.
**NEAREST TOWN:**
Mokolo 160 km (100 mi)
**YOU SHOULD KNOW:**
Visitors are obliged to take a guide with them, and may not disembark from their vehicle.

*Giraffes crossing a road in Waza National Park.*

11

# Niokolo-Koba National Park

**WHAT IS IT?**
One of West Africa's most important wildlife reserves.
**HOW TO GET THERE:**
By road from Tambacounda via Kedougou and Dar Salam.
**WHEN TO GO:**
March to May (closed June to November)
**NEAREST TOWN:**
Tambacounda 140 km (90 mi)
**DON'T MISS:**
The chimpanzees in the area of Mount Assirik.
**YOU SHOULD KNOW:**
There is an entrance fee. You must travel in a vehicle as walking is not allowed in the park.

One of the largest national parks in West Africa, Niokolo-Koba National Park is situated in the south east of Senegal and is famous for its diverse wildlife. The park, which covers an area of over 9,000 sq km (3,474 sq mi), is home to over 80 different mammal species, including lions, leopards, elephants, buffalos, hippos and hyenas, as well as some 30 types of reptile and over 300 different bird species.

*A leopard sits proudly in Niokolo-Koba National Park.*

The landscape throughout the park is generally flat; the varied vegetation includes savannah, forests, lakes and marshes. The park is well watered as the Gambia River, along with its tributaries, the Niokolo-Koba and the Koulountou, run though it.

Included on the UNESCO list of World Heritage Sites in 1981, the park is also an international biosphere reserve. Today many of the large mammals are under threat from poaching: the numbers of leopards and elephants – the only herds remaining in Senegal – have shown significant decreases in recent years. The park's future is further threatened by several dam schemes and a road project which are under consideration in the area. While more tourists have been visiting the park of late, the numbers are still fairly modest due to the park's relative remoteness and its distance from Dakar, the capital. Potential visitors to the park may need to be reminded that, as in many wildlife reserves, though you will almost certainly see animals such as antelope and buffalo at Niokolo-Koba, sightings of lions or elephants, for example, are by no means guaranteed.

*A Green monkey mother with her baby*

# Simien National Park

Massive erosion over the years on the Ethiopian plateau has created one of the most spectacular landscapes in the world. The Simien National Park, a UNESCO World Heritage Site, consists of a rocky massif – cut through by streams and gorges – which slopes dramatically down to grasslands and wide valleys. The pinnacle of the Simien Mountains, Ras Dejen 4,620 m (15,157 ft), is the highest point in Ethiopia and the fourth highest peak on the continent.

The national park has three general botanical

*Young gelada baboons huddle together in Simien National Park.*

regions; the lower slopes for cultivation and grazing, the forested alpine regions and the higher mountain grasslands growing fescue grasses and heathers, splendid red hot pokers as well as giant lobelia.

Not only are the views from the mountains breathtaking, but the park is also home to some extremely rare animals such as the gelada (bleeding heart) baboons with their distinctive red breasts, the obscure Simien fox, Ethiopian wolves and large birds of prey including the lammergeier. The park was created primarily to protect the 1,000 walia ibex, a type of wild goat found nowhere else in the world, which also live in the park.

Trekking in the Simiens is excellent and the park is easily accessible from Debareq, 101 km (63 mi) from Gondar. The infrastructure is good: equipment, provisions and guides are available. Although not too far from the equator, snow and ice commonly appear on the highest points of the Simien Mountains and temperatures at night often fall below 0 °C (32 °F) so it is important to be prepared for all conditions.

*Following pages: the view towards the Northern Escarpment near Sankaber*

# Lake Nakuru

**WHAT IS IT?**
Home to up to 2 million
flamingos.
**HOW TO GET THERE:**
By air and/or road from
Nairobi via Nakuru.
**WHEN TO GO:**
July to February.
**NEAREST TOWN:**
Nakuru 5 km (3 mi)
**YOU SHOULD KNOW:**
The best vantage point to
view the flamingos is
Baboon Cliff. Nakuru means
'dust' or 'dusty place' in the
Maasai language.

Less than 160 km (100 mi) from Nairobi, Kenya's
capital city, Lake Nakuru is world famous for the huge
number of flamingos that inhabit its shores. The
extraordinary sight of the continually shifting mass of
pink created by often more than a million flamingos on
the lake is truly breathtaking.

The flamingos are attracted by the algae that thrive
in the shallow, warm and strongly alkaline waters of
the lake. Scientists estimate that the flamingos
consume as much as 250,000 kg (551,200 lbs) of algae
per hectare per year. In the dry season the lake's area
reduces to little more than 5 sq km (2 sq mi) but the
rains increase it to about 45 sq km (17 sq mi) and the

flamingo population on the lake varies accordingly.
Pelicans and cormorants are also common and there
are thought to be over 400 resident bird species on the
lake and in the surrounding park.

In recent years the flamingo population has
decreased alarmingly partly as a result of intensive
crop production in the surrounding area and the
increased water usage in nearby Nakuru, which is
Kenya's fourth largest city.

The lake and the surrounding area was designated
Lake Nakuru National Park in the 1960s and later
enlarged to some 190 sq km (73 sq mi) as well as
being fenced off primarily to protect the populations of
Rothschild giraffes, and the black and white rhinos
which have been introduced to the park. It is the only
fully fenced national park in Kenya.

*A group of flamingos in
the shallow waters of
Lake Nakuru*

# Amboseli National Park

Amboseli National Park has been under the control of the Olkejiado County Council, rather than the Kenyan Wildlife Service, since September 2005. This change means that revenue generated by the park now benefits the local Maasai communities.

Amboseli is one of Kenya's most popular wildlife-viewing sites and is renowned for its population of an estimated 650 elephants, as well as its large herds of wildebeest, zebra, impala and, if you're lucky, the endangered black rhino and elusive cheetah. The backdrop of the snow-capped peak of Mount Kilimanjaro, just 40 km (25 mi) away and rising majestically above the clouds, dominates the reserve.

Designated an international biosphere reserve and national park in 1974, Amboseli covers a mere 392 sq km (244 sq mi), but despite its small size and the

fragility of its ecosystem, it manages to support a wide range of mammals. More than 50 of the larger species of mammals and over 400 species of birds can be found throughout the area.

With its rugged landscape and the romantic, mystical atmosphere of the great mountain looming above, it is no wonder that Amboseli inspired the big-game-hunting

tales of Ernest Hemingway and Robert Ruark.

The volcanic ash from Kilimanjaro's last eruption thousands of years ago gives many areas of the reserve a dusty appearance, yet a continuous supply of water from the mountain's melted snow flows in underground streams creating the bold contrast of lush green areas. Various springs, swamps and marshes in the park provide havens for wildlife.

Keep an eye out for the arid lakebed that produces mirages in the sweltering heat and be sure to enjoy the views afforded by Observation Hill.

*A herd of African Elephants*

*Left: An aerial view of elephants crossing the park*

*Following pages: Zebras beneath Kilimanjaro*

21

# Tsingy of Bemaraha

**WHAT IS IT?**
A reserve with a unique 'forest' of limestone pinnacles.
**HOW TO GET THERE:**
Flights from Antananarivo to Antsalova then by road (4 wheel drive)
**WHEN TO GO:**
July to October.
**NEAREST TOWN:**
Morondava 225 km (140 mi)
**DON'T MISS:**
The ancient cemeteries in the Manambolo Gorge. The avenues of Baobab trees near Morondava.
**YOU SHOULD KNOW:**
There are no facilities within the reserve. The nearest hotel is 150 km (94 mi) away. Road travel is slow and arduous.

Located some 80 km (50 mi) inland from Madagascar's west coast, much of this reserve is a mass of sharp-ridged limestone pinnacles – 'tsingy' in the Malagasy language – some rising up to heights of 50 m (160 ft) and cut through with canyons and gorges. Declared a nature reserve in 1927, this extraordinary mineral 'forest' was recognized as a UNESCO World Heritage Site in 1990 and opened, in part, to the public as recently as 1998.

These peculiar rock formations, which are unique to Madagascar, were created by erosion as the acidity of rainwater over the centuries gradually dissolved the stone of the chalky plateau. The pinnacles are so close together as to make the area virtually impenetrable by humans; yet there are many species of lemur here whose agility is entirely unaffected by the razor-sharp stone environment.

The eastern border of the reserve is defined by the Bemaraha Cliff, which rises dramatically some 400 m (1,300 ft) above the Manambolo River valley. The northern part, which is closed to the public, is a mixture of undulating hills and limestone extrusions.

Madagascar is famous for its unique diversity of wildlife – nearly 90 per cent of the species to be found on this beautiful island, the world's fourth largest, can only be found here – and the Tsingy of Bemaraha reserve itself is the only known location for a number of rare plants and animals, some of which are endangered. There are numerous springs at the base of the pinnacles and the Tsingy provides an important water catchment function for the surrounding area, particularly to the west.

*An aerial view of the stunning limestone pinnacles*

# Rwanda – Parc National des Volcans

Known everywhere as the place where Dian Fossey, the eminent primatologist, spent years studying the habits and habitats of the rare mountain gorillas, the Parc National des Volcans is truly a must-see.

In the heart of Central Africa, on the steep, lush slopes of north-west Rwanda, the diverse ecosystems of the Congo basin meet the great rift valleys of the west, creating a rich biodiversity not found anywhere else on the continent.

As you trek through evergreen and bamboo forest and open grassland, at the foothills of the scenic Virungas mountains – encompassing six volcanoes – traversing rivers and streams that flow into the Nile, you walk up, up, up towards where the rainforest converges with the rest of this green, tropical paradise. It is here you will find yourself cloaked in the heart of the Parc National des Volcans – or Volcano National Park.

Nearly 4,572 m (15,000 ft) from the forest bed, this is the home to the rare mountain gorilla. As your guide leads you towards the gorillas, you will be surrounded by the sounds of bird calls – more than 670 species are found here – and the squawking and haunting noises of monkeys climbing above you, while getting an occasional peek of a buffalo or elephant. You will find yourself holding your breath as you walk silently on fallen leaves, hoping to catch an up-close glimpse of a silverback gorilla.

At three times the weight of an average grown man, these gentle giants are surprisingly tolerant of their human guests, so long as the latter follow the rules about maintaining their distance and keeping quiet. Meeting these beautiful creatures is certainly an experience that will not be forgotten!

**WHAT IS IT?**
The national park renowned for Dian Fossey's study of its gorilla population. It is home to nearly 400 rare mountain gorillas.

**HOW TO GET THERE:**
Ruhengeri is a 90-minute drive from Rwanda's capital city, Kigali.

**WHEN TO GO:**
It is possible to track mountain gorillas year-round but visiting during the dry season between June and September is best.

**NEAREST TOWN:**
Ruhengeri

**YOU SHOULD KNOW:**
If you intend to make a gorilla visit, you will need to organize transport from Ruhengeri town to the park boundaries, where you will continue your guided trip on foot. For the protection of the gorillas, access is limited to a handful of people a day, and there are strict rules about how to behave near the gorillas. The area is also known as the Land of a Thousand Hills.

*A family of mountain gorillas*

27

# Ngorongoro Conservation Area

**WHAT IS IT?**
The largest intact volcanic caldera on Earth.
**HOW TO GET THERE:**
By road from Kilimanjaro International Airport.
**WHEN TO GO:**
The wildlife is always spectacular, but is particularly special during the migration season in December and June.
**NEAREST TOWN:**
Arusha 190 km (120 mi)
**DON'T MISS:**
A guided walking safari.

Centred around the collapsed crater of an ancient volcano in the southern part of the Great Rift Valley, the Ngorongoro Conservation Area is a stunningly beautiful landscape that holds a fantastic range of wildlife. There are good populations of lion and cheetah, as well as resident wildebeest, zebra, eland, Grant's and Thomson's gazelles, mountain reedbuck, hippo, black rhino, hartebeest, elephant, spotted hyena, jackal and buffalo. Twice a year, millions of migrants pass through on their way to and from the Serengeti, following the rains that bring fresh pasture. More than 550 species of birds have been seen in the park, with the flamingos of Lake Magadi being perhaps the most special.

The huge crater formed some two million years ago when the volcano erupted violently and its magma chamber collapsed, creating the largest unbroken volcanic caldera in the world, with a maximum diameter of 22.5 km (14 mi) and a depth of 610 m (2,000 ft).

In the wider park, there are more mountains, including several active volcanoes, forests, lakes and wide plains. In the north are the Maasai sacred mountain, Oldoinya Lengai, the Olduvai Gorge where

some of the earliest remains of modern man (*Homo habilis*) as well as early man (*Paranthropus boisei*) were discovered and the soda lake, Lake Natron, where thousands of pink flamingos breed on little mud mounds.

A visit to this remote park, with its awe-inspiring landscapes and plentiful wildlife, is a must-see for any lover of wildlife.

*Zebra and wildebeest herds in Ngorongoro Crater*

# Mgahinga Gorilla National Park

Despite being the smallest of Uganda's National Parks, Mgahinga, at 33.7 sq km (13 sq mi), is still one of the most important. It adjoins both Rwanda's Parc

des Volcans and the Democratic Republic of Congo's Virunga National Park. The Virunga Mountains are a series of both active and extinct volcanoes that straddle the border of these three countries, three of which (all extinct) can be climbed in Mgahinga.

Mgahinga is famous for its tiny population of endangered Mountain gorillas, including one family consisting of nine animals (including two silverbacks and three adult females) that are familiarized with tracking. This family often moves across the border into Rwanda, and therefore gorilla-tracking safaris can only be confirmed a short time in advance. Groups from the neighbouring countries sometimes visit the area for a month or two.

The tropical rainforest that covers the lower slopes has been somewhat depleted for farmland, but higher up there are abundant bamboo and Alpine forests. Largely vegetarian, male Mountain gorillas weigh as much as 195 kg (430 lbs) and can eat up to 34 kg (75 lbs) of vegetation each day. Gallium vines form a large part of their diet but they also love bamboo shoots, moving down to the bamboo forests when new shoots are available. They will also climb up to sub-alpine regions in order to eat another delicacy, the soft centre of the giant Senecio tree.

Mountain gorillas are almost extinct. There are thought to be between 650 and 700 animals left in the world, shared between these three countries. One of two sub-species of gorilla, they have longer, darker hair than other gorillas, enabling them to live at higher, colder altitudes. These charming, fascinating creatures are endangered by habitat loss, poaching and disease, particularly human diseases such as colds and flu to which they have no immunity.

**WHAT IS IT?**
Uganda's smallest national park, home to the Mountain gorilla.
**HOW TO GET THERE:**
By road from Kampala, or fly to Kisoro and then go by road.
**WHEN TO GO:**
June, July, August or January.
**NEAREST TOWN:**
Kisoro 10 km (6 mi)
**DON'T MISS:**
The view from the top of Mount Muhavura.
**YOU SHOULD KNOW:**
Gorilla tracking permits are in high demand, so organize your trip and permit several months in advance.

*Silverback mountain gorilla*

# Cape Cross Seal Reserve

**WHAT IS IT?**
A breeding area for between 80,000 and 100,000 of Cape Fur Seals.

**HOW TO GET THERE:**
The turnoff to the reserve is signposted on the C34, 120km (75 mi) north of Swakopmund.

**WHEN TO GO:**
The breeding season, including birth and the next rutting, takes place in November and December.

**NEAREST TOWN:**
The coastal fishing town of Henties Bay.

**YOU SHOULD KNOW:**
There is no accommodation in this area – stay at either Henties Bay or Swakopmund.

The Cape Fur Seal is the largest of the world's nine species of fur seals, and they are, in fact, a species of sea lion. Along the Namibian and South African coastline, there are as many as 650,000 fur seals in the 24 colonies. Cape Cross Seal Reserve in Namibia is the largest breeding area, with a population of between 80,000 and 100,000 seals.

The bulls, or males, arrive at the colony in October and, after marking their territories, will fiercely defend them. The pregnant cows, or females, usually arrive at the colony in November. Each will give birth to one pup and become fertile again in a single week – this is when the 'rutting' season begins.

A bull, hosting between five and 25 cows in his territory during any one mating season, loses an incredible amount of his original 360 kg (794 lbs) weight defending his territory against his fellow bulls. The young fur seals are born pitch black, weighing 5–7 kg (11–15.5 lb) each. They suckle immediately after birth, and will continue to do so for nearly a year. They will supplement their mother's milk with fish when they reach about five months. The mothers continue to feed at sea while their pups are on shore and it is during this time, when their young are left alone on the shore in the colony, that they are sometimes eaten

by black-backed jackals or brown hyenas. One out of four pups born at the colony will not survive infancy.

*Cape Fur Seals*

The warm-blooded fur seals are able to withstand the waters of the frigid Benguela Current because of their many layers of blubber and special double-layered fur coats. Although the fish they subsist on are not commercially caught species, many fishermen still consider the seals to be a threat to the fishing industry.

Witnessing the spectacle of such an enormous number of these beautiful creatures in their natural habitat is certainly worth the day trip from Henties Bay or Swakopmund.

# iSimangaliso Wetland Park

The iSimangaliso Wetland Park, formerly known as Greater St Lucia Wetland Park, on the east coast of KwaZulu-Natal, is arguably the finest nature reserve in a country that boasts some of the richest and most exciting wildlife in the world.

What makes South Africa's third-largest protected area such a living treasure is that within its boundaries lies a unique combination of ecosystems, ranging from open sea to estuary, sand dunes to swamps – and all surrounding the shimmering waters of Lake St Lucia.

The Indian Ocean acts as the park's eastern border. Humpback whales and great white shark swim here, as do coelacanths, living relics from 400 million years ago. Nearer the shore you will find the underwater splendour of Africa's most southerly coral reefs, thanks to the warming effect of the Agulhas Current.

Moving inland over the sandy beaches, where leatherback and loggerhead turtles come to lay their eggs, there is the tallest forested coastal dune system in the world. Of the larger mammals that live here, reedbuck are the most numerous, but a few black rhino may also be seen.

Further west lie the park's shimmering lakes, translucent blue jewels splashed with the pink and white of flamingos and pelicans.

Hippos live here too – around 800 of them. For

*Beach and forested dunes near Mabibi*

much of the day they laze about in the water. By night, however, they come ashore to graze the grassy banks in grumbling herds.

More numerous still are the Nile crocodiles. Great care needs to be taken around these formidable 5 m- (16 ft-) long predators, and the St Lucia Crocodile Centre is the best place for visitors seeking close encounters of the crocodilian kind.

Comprising an awesome 3,280 sq km (1,266 sq mi), iSimangaliso Wetland Park is without doubt a wildlife wonderland. No wonder then that in 1999 it was also declared a World Heritage Site.

# Lapalala Wilderness

The lyrically named Lapalala Wilderness lies within the UNESCO Waterberg Biosphere Reserve, in Limpopo Province, just a three and a half hours' drive from Johannesburg. Despite its name, Lapalala is actually a privately owned nature reserve, created from the consolidation of 19 farms between 1981 and

*Black rhinoceros*

1999. Currently some 360 sq km (140 sq mi) in extent, there are plans to extend the reserve still further.

The Lapalala Wilderness is characterized by endless vistas of upland plains and rugged hills, dissected by craggy ravines. The predominant vegetation here is so-called bushveld – grassland, punctuated by dense clusters of trees and tall shrubs. Bringing the whole area to life are the 90 km (56 mi) or so of rivers and streams that course through it, chief of which is the Palala River with its clear pools and noisy rapids.

Within this largely unspoiled landscape, visitors can encounter the wildlife both from the seat of a Land Rover, or by foot on guided walks. There are buffalo, hippo, crocodile, zebra, leopard, baboons and many kinds of antelope here as well as over 280 species of bird.

But Lapalala's 'A-list' is without doubt its black and white rhino. Hunted dangerously close to extinction, both species have only been saved by the strenuous efforts of conservationists such as Lapalala's Clive Walker.

Black and white rhino are easy to tell apart – but not for the reason suggested by their names. Black rhino (*Diceros bicornis*) are the smaller species and have a hooked upper lip, which they use to grasp the leaves and shoots that they eat. White rhino, (*Cerototherium simum*) by contrast, have very wide mouths, which they use to tear off great mouthfuls of grass. It was a corruption of the word 'wide' which in Afrikaans sounds like 'white', that led to them being called white rhino, when in reality they are much the same colour as black rhino.

To be able to have a close encounter with both these species in a single day leaves visitors with memories to last a lifetime and makes Lapalala a truly special place.

**WHAT IS IT?**
A privately owned game reserve.
**HOW TO GET THERE:**
By road or bus from Johannesburg.
**WHEN TO GO:**
There is plenty to see all year.
**NEAREST TOWN:**
Vaalwater 50 km (30 mi) to the south west.
**DON'T MISS:**
The Waterberg Environmental Centre, Melkrivier.
**YOU SHOULD KNOW:**
There is a charge to enter the reserve. Game drives and guided walks may need advance booking.

*Following pages: A stunning view of Lapalala Camp from Lookout, with Malore Hill in the background*

# The MalaMala Reserve

**WHAT IS IT?**
A privately owned game reserve.
**HOW TO GET THERE:**
By air from Johannesburg to MalaMala Airfield, or by road from Johannesburg.
**WHEN TO GO:**
There is plenty to see all year. September to March can be very hot.
**NEAREST TOWN:**
Newington 19 km (12 mi) west.
**YOU SHOULD KNOW:**
To visit MalaMala you must be resident in one of the reserve's lodges. The area is malarial so take precautions.

The MalaMala Game Reserve is a 160 sq km (62 sq mi) wildlife sanctuary located in Mpumalanga Province. Established in 1927, MalaMala lays claim to being the oldest game reserve in South Africa. At one time it was a hunter's paradise for those seeking to bag the 'Big Five', but since 1964 the only shooting that has been done here has been done by tourists with cameras.

Much of MalaMala is textbook African savannah, replete with an impressive inventory of wildlife species – the richest anywhere on the continent. If that were not enough, MalaMala holds further aces that make it one of the premier game viewing destinations in the world.

First is its sheer size, guaranteeing visitors a rich and varied habitat. Second is the fact that it fortuitously shares a 19 km (12 mi) unfenced border with the Kruger National Park. This simple accident of geography benefits the reserve enormously. Thirdly, MalaMala is blessed with the life-giving waters of the Sand River. Some 20 km (13 mi) of this perennial river flows north-south through the reserve, drawing huge herds of grazing animals to its banks – not to mention the numerous predators that hunt them.

To allow the animals approaching from the Kruger National Park free access to the river, all the MalaMala camps are on the western bank, and throughout the reserve human density and impact on the land is kept to an absolute minimum.

The results of this single-minded management are obvious in the reserve's viewing statistics. Typically, lion, leopard, elephant, rhino and buffalo make an appearance here 335 days every year. So for visitors on a once-in-a-lifetime trip to see Africa's 'Big Five', MalaMala is unlikely to disappoint.

Visitors staying on the reserve are provided with their own personal guide and local Shangaan trackers. These experts know the area and its inhabitants intimately. Whether by open top Land Rover or on foot – with an armed ranger – by day or night, these guides will help guarantee an unforgettable experience not least of which is an unrivalled opportunity to photograph the best of Africa's wildlife.

*A lion in the MalaMala Reserve, the oldest game reserve in South Africa*

# AMERICAS &
# THE CARIBBEAN

# Wood Buffalo National Park

**WHAT IS IT?**
Home to the largest herd of bison in North America, and the only nesting grounds of the whooping crane.
**HOW TO GET THERE:**
By plane from Edmonton to Fort Smith, then by plane or by road.
**NEAREST TOWN:**
Hay River, adjacent to the park or Fort Smith in the NWT, 280 km (175mi)
**YOU SHOULD KNOW:**
There are 36 campsites in the park, but only one is accessible by road. Park offices are located in Fort Smith and Fort Chipewyan.

Wood Buffalo National Park was established in 1922. It is located on the boundary between Alberta and the Northwest Territories, and was designated a UNESCO World Heritage Site in 1983. It was created specifically to protect North America's largest free-roaming bison herd, some 2,500 animals, but it also contains the only natural nesting grounds of the critically endangered whooping crane.

Wood Buffalo is Canada's largest national park, a boreal forest zone covering 44,807 sq km (17,300 sq mi). Within its boundaries there are fire-scarred forested uplands, a glacially eroded plateau, a major freshwater delta formed by three major rivers, salt plains and some of the best examples of karst topography in North America. It also contains the largest undisturbed grass and sedge meadows in North America, making ideal bison country.

The park has the longest tradition of native subsistence use in the country. It has been inhabited since the glaciers retreated, most recently by nomadic Micasew-Cree First Nation groups, some of whom still fish, hunt and trap here. The climate is one of long, cold winters and short, warm summers, and it is only frost-free in June, July and August.

There are 47 species of mammal here, including caribou, arctic fox, black bear, moose, beaver and muskrat, and 227 bird species have been recorded, including peregrine falcon, bald eagles, great grey and snowy owls. The bison are self-regulating and it is one of the few places left in the world where a genuine predator-versus-prey relationship exists between wolves and bison. The whooping cranes number some 140 individuals, of which there are 40 breeding pairs. The careful management and protection of these birds within the park, and the protection of their winter grounds in Texas, may have saved them from extinction.

*An aerial view of Wood Buffalo National Park*

# Algonquin Provincial Park

**WHAT IS IT?**
One of Canada's largest provincial parks.

**HOW TO GET THERE:**
The park is immediately east of Muskoka in Ontario. The main access points are via Highway 60, east of Huntsville.

**WHEN TO GO:**
From July to the end of September

**NEAREST TOWN:**
Deep River in the Ottawa Valley region of Eastern Ontario and to the northwest is the town of North Bay.

**DON'T MISS:**
You can canoe in the 1,610 km (1,000 mi) or so of canoe routes, hike the backpacking trails, ride a mountain bike, cross-country ski, fish or birdwatch.

**YOU SHOULD KNOW:**
It inspired the famous Group of Seven Artists.

Algonquin Provincial Park in Ontario encompasses 7,725 sq km (4,800 sq mi) of forests, lakes and rivers, reminiscent of wilderness from a vanishing past. The park is set in a transition zone amid both deciduous and coniferous forests, with a lush landscape of maples, spruce bogs, beaver ponds, lakes and wildflower-strewn cliffs, each of which provides ample opportunities to see a wide array of plants and wildlife not commonly found together.

Within the park's boundaries you will find 53 species of mammals, 272 species of birds, 31 species of reptiles and amphibians, 54 species of fish and roughly 7,000 species of insects! More than 1,000 species of plants, as well as more

than 1,000 species of fungi are also found here.

Originally inhabited by aboriginals who came here to fish, hunt and pick berries, the rugged Algonquin highlands were not settled by pioneers until the nineteenth century when loggers arrived from the Ottawa Valley in search of white pines whose wood was increasingly in demand by a growing British economy.

Algonquin Provincial Park was established in 1893 as a wildlife sanctuary to protect the headwaters of the five major rivers that flow from the park. Eventually this area of majestic beauty was 'discovered' by adventurous fishermen, then by Tom Thomson and the famous Canadian landscape painters, the Group of Seven, and a host of other visitors. People travel from around the world to hear the howls of wolves echoing in the beautiful area, as well as to catch sight of the moose that inhabit the park in large numbers.

*Morning frost in Algonquin Provincial Park*

# Gros Morne National Park

**WHAT IS IT?**
An area of extraordinary natural beauty
**HOW TO GET THERE:**
By a combination of plane, ferry, car or bus.
**WHEN TO GO:**
Any time, weather permitting, but from May to October an entry fee is payable.
**NEAREST TOWN:**
Deer Lake 32 km (20 mi) from the park entrance or Rocky Harbour, in the Park itself.
**DON'T MISS:**
The rhododendrons in spring and the autumn colours.
**YOU SHOULD KNOW:**
Fascinating boat trips are available – enjoy the stunning coastline and, if you are very lucky, spot a whale.

The island of Newfoundland is the easternmost part of Canada and, situated on its rugged west coast, is Gros Morne National Park – part of the Long Range Mountains that stretch the whole length of that side of the island. The mountains here are the weathered remains of a range formed some thousand million years ago, making them 20 times older than the Rocky Mountains of western Canada. The range resulted from a continental collision and during the last three million years, 30 periods of glaciation have occurred. As the ice came and went, the peaks wore down to the rounded summits that we see today.

Gros Morne National Park is an area of extraordinary natural beauty. It was declared a UNESCO World Heritage Site in 1987 not only for its visual impact but also because its topography reveals the major stages of the evolutionary history of the planet. Possibly its most spectacular feature is Western Brook Pond, a 30 km (19 mi) long fjord-like structure formed by the same glacial action that produced Norway's fjords. Western Brook Pond, however, was later cut off from the ocean, and is filled with pure, fresh, dark-blue water that cascades from

the plateau above it. Pissing Mare Falls, the highest falls in eastern North America, flow into it.

Another unique feature, known as the Tablelands, is a 600 m- (1,950 ft-) high plateau made of rock from the earth's mantle that was forced to the surface hundreds of millions of years ago. It is a mysterious and barren area, hardly able to support plant life. Elsewhere the park has a wide variety of habitat from coastal lowlands to wooded mountains, supporting 14 species of land mammal, including black bear, lynx, caribou and arctic hare.

*Evening light on coastal cliffs at Neddies Harbour*

# Niagara Falls

Although they are not the highest or broadest falls in the world, Niagara are the best known. Lying across the border between Canada and the United States, they were formed towards the end of the last ice age, when the glaciers of the Laurentide ice sheet retreated creating the Great Lakes. Water flowing from Lake Erie to Lake Ontario carved a gorge past the Niagara escarpment and over the millennia since, it has eroded the shale below the hard dolomitic rock at the top. The falls are currently retreating at a rate of about 1 m (3 ft) a year.

On the American side of the border, the Niagara falls carry about 10 per cent of the flow, while on the Canadian side the Horseshoe falls carry far more. The water flows at the astonishing rate of 56.3 kph (35 mph).

The local tribespeople call the falls 'onguiaahra', a 'thundering noise', which may seem like an understatement when you are faced with the sheer noise of almost 185,000 cubic m (6,600,00 cubic ft) of water roaring into the gorge every minute.

The *Maid of the Mist* takes visitors up the gorge to the base of the Horseshoe falls for a truly dramatic, and wet, experience and photogenic views as the sun creates rainbows in the mists.

*Water rushing over
Horseshoe Falls*

# Olympic National Park

The Olympic Peninsula protrudes into the Pacific Ocean at the far north western tip of Washington State, just to the south of Vancouver Island. Almost all of it is designated wilderness and Olympic National Park covers 373,347 hectares (922,561 acres), having become an International Biosphere Reserve in 1976 and a World Heritage Site in 1981.

The Park naturally divides into three areas: the Pacific coastline, temperate rainforest and the Olympic Mountains that separate the peninsula from the land to the south. This isolation has resulted in many endemic flora and fauna, such as the Olympic marmot, as well as endangered species such as the Northern Spotted owl and Marbled Murrelet. The mountains are topped with ancient glaciers, with the 2,428 m (7,965 ft) peak of Mount Olympus dominating the western half.

The temperate rainforest is in the west of the park, which receives more rain than anywhere

**WHAT IS IT?**
A national park containing three distinct ecosystems.
**HOW TO GET THERE:**
By bus or ferry to Port Angeles, then by car and on foot.
**WHEN TO GO:**
July to September.
**NEAREST TOWN:**
Port Angeles, on the northern edge of the Park.

*Left: Sol Duc Falls cascading through rainforest.*

*Moss-covered trees in Olympic National Park*

*Crescent Lake*

else in the country, with the exception of Kauai in Hawaii. This is an amazing area of old growth forest, dense with Sitka spruce, western hemlock, Douglas fir, cedar, maple, alder and black cottonwood, producing habitat for many different creatures.

The coastal area is wild and wonderful, with some sandy beaches often covered with logs and other flotsam and others covered with great lumps of rock. There are arches and sea stacks, tide pools full of shells and other marine life, and birds such as Oyster catchers and Bald eagles. There are still a few Native American communities living in this marvellous wilderness, and several roads enter the park, though none penetrate far, leaving the interior only accessible by trail.

# Cadillac Mountain, Acadia National Park, Maine

Acadia National Park, off Maine's Atlantic coast, comprises Mount Desert Island, parts of three smaller, neighbouring islands, and some of the mainland's Schoodic Peninsula. Mount Desert Island contains seventeen mountains, including the famous Cadillac Mountain.

Cadillac Mountain is formed of pink granite, and covered with pitch pine and spruce forests. Its summit, between October 7th and March 6th of every year, is thought to be the first place in the USA to receive the sun's rays. From here, on a clear day, it is possible to see both Nova Scotia, lying over 160 km (100 mi) to the east and, at a similar distance to the north, Maine's highest peak, Mount Katahdin. Views over the park itself are utterly delightful, and can be explored in greater detail by following the glorious 43 km- (27 mi-) long, one-way Park Loop Road.

The park is unique in that it exists largely thanks to private citizens who, realizing the dangers of over development, helped to create it. President Woodrow

**WHAT IS IT?**
The only national park in New England.
**HOW TO GET THERE:**
A causeway links Mount Desert Island to the mainland.
**WHEN TO GO:**
Open all year, but the best weather is in July and August.
**NEAREST TOWN:**
There are three towns on Mount Desert Island itself, Bar Harbor, Southwest Harbor and Northeast Harbor.
**DON'T MISS:**
Sunrise from the summit of Cadillac Mountain.
**YOU SHOULD KNOW:**
At 471 m (1,532ft) high, Cadillac Mountain is the highest peak on the eastern seaboard.

*Beautiful autumn colours in Acadia National Park*

Wilson designated it a National Monument in 1916, and in 1929 it was named Acadia. It remains a tribute to John D. Rockefeller Jr., who not only donated about a third of the land but was also responsible for designing more than 80 km (50 mi) of carriage trails through the park, as well as seventeen granite bridges and two gate lodges.

The park contains a mass of wildlife – 40 types of mammal, marine life including seals and off-shore whales and over 300 species of birds, almost half of them breeding pairs, including peregrine falcons. These magnificent raptors are endangered but several pairs of chicks have been successfully raised here during the past fifteen years.

*Bass Harbor Marsh*

# Autumn colours of New England

**WHAT IS IT?**
One of nature's most colourful spectacles.
**HOW TO GET THERE:**
By road from anywhere on the US eastern seaboard, from Maryland northwards to Vermont.
**WHEN TO GO:**
Early October is the most reliable time.
**YOU SHOULD KNOW:**
The timing for the change in leaf colour is dependent on the weather.

Every October, the leaves in New England burst into a spectacular symphony of vibrant colours before they fall to the ground as the trees become dormant for winter, and 'tree peeping' is a common pastime here during the autumn. Once you see the joyous explosion of colours bursting over the picturesque landscape, you will understand why this is the most popular season for visiting the area.

So why do leaves change colour in autumn? At this time of year the production of chlorophyll in leaves stops and so they lose their vibrant green colours revealing the underlying tones caused by the presence of other pigments, such as carotenoids which provide yellow, orange and brown colours and anthocyanins which give red and purple colours.

Autumn leaf colour is specific to the species of tree because of the different chemicals in the leaves. Oaks turn red, brown, or russet; hickories become golden bronze; dogwoods go purplish red; beech fade to light tan; red maple turn a brilliant scarlet; sugar maple go orange-red; black maple become glowing yellow;

*Autumn colours in Connecticut*

sourwood and black tupelo change to crimson and aspen, birch, and yellow poplar turn a golden yellow.

The range and intensity of autumn colours are greatly influenced by the weather and the brightest autumn colours are produced when dry, sunny days are followed by cool, dry nights.

Regardless of timing, if you are fortunate enough to see the stunning autumn colours that cover vast swathes of New England you will understand why there is even a foliage hot line offering hourly reports on the best places to go.

*Following pages:Woodland in Vermont*

# The Giant Redwoods of California

Giant Redwood trees, or Sequoias, are the largest trees in the world, and possibly the largest living organisms on the planet. Members of the yew family, there are three distinct species: Giant redwood, Coastal redwood and Dawn redwood. The first two types are to be found in California, and the last is native to China.

Sequoias only grow in the Sierra Nevada Mountains, and are a breath-taking sight. Humboldt Redwood State Park contains the last virgin redwood groves in the world, and is both a World Heritage Site and part of an International Biosphere reserve. These trees are up to 3,000 years old, and grow to a height of over 91 m (300 ft) reaching up through the mist and fog of California's coastal climate to tower over the surrounding forest of firs and pines. The largest tree of all is named General Sherman, and in 2002 it was measured at 112.6 m (369 ft 6 in).

Sequoias are not only tall, they are also broad: the trunk of Shrine Drive Through Tree can indeed be driven through, and Tharp's Log is a cabin built in one, fallen, hollowed out tree. Roads wind up into the Giant Forest where a museum provides information about the trees and the efforts being made to protect them. The grandeur of these remarkable trees is truly one of nature's wonders. The lofty tranquillity of these groves gives the visitor a feeling of awe in the knowledge that the Sequoias will still be standing here long after we have gone.

**WHAT IS IT?**
The home of the world's largest trees.
**HOW TO GET THERE:**
By road along Highway 101
**WHEN TO GO:**
Open all year.
**NEAREST TOWN:**
Visalia 78 km (49 mi)
**DON'T MISS:**
Kings Canyon National Park.
**YOU SHOULD KNOW:**
An entrance fee is payable.

*Left: Redwood trees tower over the Rockefeller Loop at Humboldt Redwood State Park*

*Avenue of the Giants*

# Monument Valley

*Eye of the Sun arch*

Monument Valley is an area of sandstone rock formations rising majestically up to 300 m (1,000 ft) from the desert floor, providing one of the most enduring images of the American West. These isolated red mesas and buttes, surrounded by vast, empty desert, have been filmed and photographed countless times, giving the visitor a sense of familiarity, but once in the valley you cannot fail to be amazed at the true vivid, deep, rich colour palette of this other-worldly landscape.

Lying entirely within the Navajo Indian Reservation near the south-eastern corner of Utah, the most famous landmarks are concentrated around the small town of Goulding. This isolated settlement, 250 km (175 mi) from the nearest city – Flagstaff, Arizona – was

established in 1923 as an Indian trading post, and is now home to a comprehensive range of visitor services.

The view from the visitor centre is spectacular enough, but the majority of the park can only be seen from the Valley Drive, a 27-km (17-mi) road. Winding among the magical towering cliffs and mesas including The Totem Pole, a stunning 91-m (300-ft) rock spire only a few metres wide. As well as eroded rocks, this area is also home to a series of ancient cave and cliff dwellings, natural arches and petroglyphs.

Not a valley in the conventional sense, Monument Valley is actually a wide flat, desolate landscape, interrupted by the crumbling formations, the final remnants of the sandstone layers that once covered the entire region. Monument Valley is the quintessential, spectacular, breathtaking Wild West.

**NEAREST TOWN:**
Kayenta, 32 km (20 mi)
**YOU SHOULD KNOW:**
Monument Valley is a Navajo Indian Tribal Park, not a national park, and an entrance fee is payable. Access on the reservation is very restricted. Do not take pictures of the Native Americans or their property without permission, and, if permission is granted, expect to pay a tip.

*John Ford Point looks out over the valley*

*Following pages: The Mittens at sunset*

# Grand Canyon

**WHAT IS IT?**
One of the seven natural wonders of the world - 322 km (200 mi) of stunning landscape.

**HOW TO GET THERE:**
Highway 64 or rail from Williams.

**WHEN TO GO:**
The south rim is open all year, but is busy in summer. The north rim is shut from mid-October to mid-May. The lower reaches of the canyon are extremely hot in summer.

**NEAREST TOWN:**
Williams 95 km (60 mi)

**DON'T MISS:**
A mule ride into the canyon.

**YOU SHOULD KNOW:**
The Skywalk viewing platform is over a side canyon off the north side of the river, and is accessible only by a shuttle bus trip from Grand Canyon West or as part of a tour package.

The Grand Canyon, cut by the Colorado River, is one of the United State's most famous landmarks and stretches an incredible 322 km (200 mi) across the desert highlands of northern Arizona. Named as one of the seven natural wonders of the world, the Grand Canyon was designated a National Park in 1919.

Here you will find a breathtaking chasm of unimaginable scope in a palette of crimson, gold and orange cliffs, purple abysses and clear rushing waters, making it one of the most astonishing landscapes on Earth. Upon seeing the drama of a Grand Canyon sunset, the poet Carl Sandburg remarked, 'There goes God with an army of banners'.

*Grand Canyon bathed in sunlight*

The southern rim of the Grand Canyon is the most popular area because it allows easy access from the main road that parallels the canyon edge for a substantial distance and has many scenic overlooks as well as a selection of hiking trails.

The north rim, higher in elevation, is less densely populated with tourists because it is more remote. On this side of the canyon, the remote Tuweep area can be reached by several dirt tracks with some spectacular viewpoints, but much of this area is inaccessible by road.

The Grand Canyon contains a large variety of spectacular but largely hidden and hard-to-reach places including waterfalls, pools, narrow ravines and oases. Many of the vast side canyons require more than a day's travel on foot from the canyon rim, or complicated journeys involving boat trips down the Colorado River, to reach them.

After one trip here, pondering the vastness of this special place, you will quickly understand its popularity and status as a natural wonder of the world.

*A view over the southern rim of the Grand Canyon*

# The Florida Everglades

The Everglades National Park, in southern Florida, is the largest protected wilderness in the south-eastern United States and was designated by President Truman in 1947 in order to protect it from land reclamation for agriculture. This stunning green marshy landscape, with wide blue skies, is also a UNESCO World Heritage Site because of the importance of the habitat and animals it shelters. It is formed by the slow movement of fresh water southwards from the Orlando Kissimmee River system via the massive Lake Okeechobee. The park protects one-fifth of the original extent of the Everglades, of which about a half remains.

The wildlife in this lush, green landscape is justifiably famous: seemingly innumerable alligators and much rarer American crocodiles sun themselves on river banks or skulk beneath the water waiting for prey; the estuaries are full of such birds as egrets, spoonbills, wood storks and herons; while the endangered manatee may be seen around the coast and in estuaries.

Although they contain both cypress and mangrove swamps, the Everglades are technically a very slow-

**WHAT IS IT?**
The largest protected wilderness area in the south-eastern US.
**HOW TO GET THERE:**
On State Road 9336 (Alligator Alley) from Florida City.
**WHEN TO GO:**
December to April is mild, relatively dry and mosquito-free.
**NEAREST TOWN:**
Florida City 15 km (9 mi)
**DON'T MISS:**
An exhilarating airboat ride.
**YOU SHOULD KNOW:**
The park headquarters is at the Ernest F. Coe Visitor Center and there are visitor centres at Everglades City, Flamingo and Shark Valley.

*An alligator in Turner River*

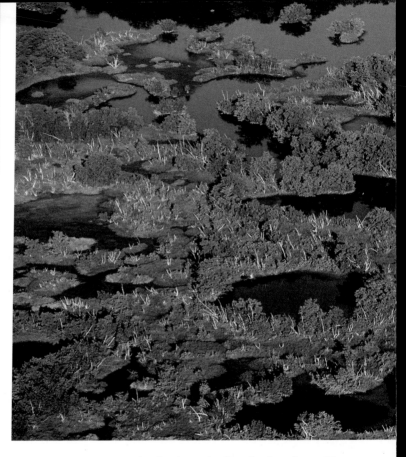

*Wetlands in the Everglades*

moving river, known locally as the river of grass: this subtropical land also has broad swathes of sawgrass and internationally important areas of rock pineland.

The main road through the park runs from Florida City on the east coast to Flamingo on the Gulf of Mexico

and is known as 'Alligator Alley' because of the hundreds of these prehistoric animals that can be seen from the road.

Short-distance walking trails, long-distance hiking routes, canoes and air boat tours allow visitors to explore this beautiful and threatened landscape.

# Sian Ka'an Biosphere

**WHAT IS IT?**
A National Biosphere Reserve & Natural World Heritage Centre.
**HOW TO GET THERE:**
By air to Cancun or Playa del Carmen.
**WHEN TO GO:**
November to May
**NEAREST TOWNS:**
Cancun, Playa del Carmen and Tulum.
**DON'T MISS:**
Chunyaxche lagoon and its surrounding *cenotes*.
**YOU SHOULD KNOW:**
There may be charges for permits to certain areas of the reserve. Check the rules for visiting different areas before you go.

The Sian Ka'an Biosphere Reserve is a 526,000 hectare (1.3 million acre) park on the eastern side of the Yucatan peninsular in the State of Quintana Roo. Set aside to preserve tropical forests, mangroves, savannas, *cenotes* (sink holes), coral reefs, and more than 25 Mayan ruins, some of it is prohibited to any kind of human access to protect its authentic pristine environment. But the majority of this huge area is a playground for some of the world's most exotic eco-tourism.

The reserve is both threatened by, and dependent on the tourist facilities between Cancun and Tulum on its northern boundary. Other than camping, it offers almost nowhere for people to stay except for a few specialist fishing lodges catering to its world-class saltwater flats fishing opportunities. Anglers can pursue bonefish, permit, barracuda and other species among the mangroves; most other visitors should take advantage of the sensitively guided tours that start from tourist centres, and visit the very best of Sian Ka'an.

Guides will take you by boat round 'islands' of

mangroves full of nesting birds, where roseate
spoonbills, ibis and tri-coloured heron are common.
Less so (but trust to luck) are jabiru, jaguars, deer,
peccaries, manatees and spider monkeys. Then,
heading inland where the salt of the lagoon turns into
the fresh water of a coastal spring, blooming orchids
and bromeliads cling to the mangrove trellis – and the
guide passes out life jackets for you to float
downstream in the cool spring water.

Of course you can drive yourself around the
reserve, stopping off to snorkel the reefs or dive in a
*cenote*. It's free to enter – but the roads will crack all
but the sturdiest axle, and finding fuel beyond Tulum
is a matter of chance.

*Skiffs anchored in a
lagoon at Sian Ka'an
Reserve.*

# Monarch Butterfly Sanctuaries

**WHAT IS IT?**
The region is an Eco-Sanctuary of international importance.
**HOW TO GET THERE:**
By car/bus from Mexico City (4hrs) W to Zitacuaro, then N to Angangueo; then by local taxi with a guide, or a tough hike N to El Rosario.
**WHEN TO GO:**
November to April.
**NEAREST TOWN:**
Angangueo 6 km (4 mi)
**YOU SHOULD KNOW:**
Take good walking shoes or boots, however you get there.
The small town of Angangueo suffered severe storm damage in February 2010.

Each November, as the North American summer ends, hundreds of millions of Monarch butterflies stream south en masse to the mountains of Michoacan, west of Mexico City. They fill the sky with a blizzard of orange and black, and settle in such dense clusters that trees sag beneath their weight. Their destination is the group of Oyamel fir forests where, at around 3,040 m (10,000 ft), they depend on a unique micro-climate to overwinter. But the area is notorious for its poverty, and the surviving forests remain under relentless threat from legal and illegal logging. Only gradually are the local co-operatives coming to understand that eco-tourism can provide them with a viable alternative income, and to support the three main Bio-Reserves of El Rosario, El Capulin, and Piedra Herrada.

The awesome spectacle of up to 250 million Monarchs is not necessarily a wilderness adventure.

The butterflies share the small pueblos and mountain villages with the farmers, schoolchildren and storekeepers who live in the forests, as well as eco-tourists. They settle everywhere, on corn-cribs, prams and street signs – even on the churches of Angangueo, the town whose steep valley and winding cobblestone lanes mark the centre of Monarch country. But you'll see them at their most

*Left and right: Monarch butterflies settling on a pine tree.*

dazzlingly prolific within the official sanctuaries. At El Rosario they carpet the forest floor in search of water, and you must step gingerly to avoid them. A sign urges you to *Guarda Silencio*: the same sign you see in Mexican churches. And it's true that the butterfly groves inspire holy awe. Sometimes, local guides feel this so strongly that they put logs across the forest trails to discourage too many visitors from exploring the groves' heart. No matter – everywhere inside the sanctuaries you will encounter rivers of butterflies streaming around you, and even stand inside their kaleidoscope of flashing brilliance.

*Following pages: The spectacular sight of Monarch butterflies flocking to branches near Angangueo.*

# Isla Carmen

**WHAT IS IT?**
The biggest island in Loreto Bay National Marine Park.
**HOW TO GET THERE:**
By air from San Diego or Los Angeles to Loreto on the Baja side of the Gulf; then by private yacht or boat charter (hiring a zodiac or skiff is recommended – anchoring is forbidden to prevent reef damage, and they are easier to beach and to swim from).
**WHEN TO GO:**
October to May; but you'll see whales by the score between January and March.
**NEAREST TOWN:**
Loreto

The Gulf of California (aka Sea of Cortez), between Baja and the Mexican mainland, is one of the world's marine marvels. Baja's 1,000 km (650 mi) spine of mountainous cactus scrub and sea pine forest guards a milk-warm oceanic playground from the violence of the Pacific. It's the southern nursery of fin, blue, sperm and orca whales, and home to countless family pods of bottlenose and common dolphins, sea lions, manta rays, and rainbow shoals of angelfish, guitarfish, redtail tigerfish and some 600 other species. Red-billed tropicbirds, blue-footed boobies, pelicans, frigatebirds and rare Heermann's gulls nesting by the thousand help to emphasize the great wildlife spectacle. And half way down the Gulf, where the temperate merges with the tropic zone, bringing together all kinds of species at their seasonal ranges in a cacophony of seabirds and

*Dolphins in the Gulf of California*

harmony of underwater song, is Isla Carmen, the biggest island in Loreto Bay National Marine Park.

Carmen used to be famous for the purity of its salt deposits, discovered in the early 16th century. Now, Salinas, its only settlement, is a ghost town among the 60 m (100 ft) cliffs, sand dunes and white beaches. Shale and gravel slope sharply to high ridges veined with dry *arroyos*. From any of Carmen's isolated coves, you lose sight of the sea in minutes, and walk in a windswept desert of giant cacti and hummingbirds. Nobody lives here, and there are no amenities. You can camp for a few days but you need prior permission (from the park authority at Loreto on the mainland) even to be there. Since commercial and big game sport fishing were banned in 1996, the ecological chain has been fully restored both on the island and in the sea: Isla Carmen's natural wealth has never been greater than in its present, splendid isolation.

**DON'T MISS:**
Getting close-up and personal to the big, barking sea lion community at Punta Lobos, a dome-shaped islet at the northern tip, connected to Carmen by a sand causeway.
Sitting low in the water in a dinghy in the company of dozens of dolphins and whales who bring their young to inspect and possibly play with you.
Star-gazing by the embers of your campfire; and waking to a fiery sunrise of molten bronze and gold – here, at least, nature is as it should be.
The view of Carmen from Loreto, itself a historical delight dating back to 1697. Loreto was the first Spanish mission in the Californias.

# Monteverde Cloud Forest

**WHAT IS IT?**
One of the most flourishing biological sanctuaries in the world.
**HOW TO GET THERE:**
By bus from either San José (4.5 hours) or Puntarenas (3 to 4 hours)
**WHEN TO GO:**
Year-round – though quieter from October to March.
**NEAREST TOWN:**
Monteverde is located near the entrance to the cloud forest.
**DON'T MISS:**
The Butterfly Garden, the Orchid Garden, the World of Insects, the Monteverde Serpentarium
**YOU SHOULD KNOW:**
If travelling with a guide ask for testimonials or get a recommendation from the local tourist authority, as some operators can be less than scrupulous. Make sure that the horses you ride look healthy and that the guide keeps to well-trodden paths.

*Following pages: Mist over the hills and rainforests of the Penas Blancas Valley*

*Tourists on a skybridge in Monteverde Cloud Forest*

Bathed in a curtain of life-giving mist, the Monteverde Cloud Forest in the mountains of Costa Rica is a profusion of saturated greenery that stands as an icon of modern day conservation. Originally founded by Quakers fleeing the draft in 1960s America, this privately owned reserve has now been expanded to cover over 10,500 hectares (26,000 acres).

With altitudes ranging between 600 m and 1,800 m (1,970 and 5,900 ft), the Forest Preserve is one of the most flourishing biological sanctuaries in the world. Over 100 species of mammals, 400 species of birds, 120 species of amphibians and reptiles, and 2,500 species of plants, as well as tens of thousands of insect species reside within its borders. In addition, larger animal species including the jaguar, ocelot, resplendent quetzal and Baird's tapir inhabit the Preserve's boundaries.

The reserve is best enjoyed at a leisurely pace and a boat trip on the adjacent Lake Arenal is a good way to get your bearings. From there it is possible to join a guided horseback trek around the lake's shores and on to Monteverde. From this vantage point you can marvel at the myriad of colours that surrounds you, whilst the sounds and scents of this most luscious of environments fills every sense. This area is a true haven for wildlife to flourish, protected from humans. It provides scientists with a great natural field station as well as delivering a wonderful, natural utopia for the more casual tourist to enjoy.

# Coiba National Park

**WHAT IS IT?**
The largest island in Central America with world-class diving.
**HOW TO GET THERE:**
By air, via Panama City, and then charter flight from various points on the mainland (the Coiba airstrip is only open to charter flights); by boat from the beach at Santa Catalina and other mainland points.

The largest – 493 sq km (310 sq mi) – island in Central America, Coiba lies 50 km (30 mi) off the Pacific coast of the Panamanian province of Veraguas. Roughly 80 per cent of it is virgin tropical rainforest, home to trees and a profusion of plants no longer found on the mainland. Throughout its hilly centre and network of rivers, thick jungle supports an unusual number of howler and white-faced capuchin monkeys, amphibians, reptiles and commonly seen, rare birds. This is where you go to see the Coiba spinetail, crested eagle, and whole flocks of gorgeous,

scarlet macaws. The macaws are the most dramatic visible evidence of the island's hitherto miraculous escape from development.

From 1919 to 2004 it was a prison colony, and even now visitors' access is restricted. In fact, in the interests of protecting Coiba's pristine ecosystem, organized tours currently offer the lowest-impact form of tourism – and help to frustrate opportunities for poaching, illegal logging and other encroachments.

Although visiting Coiba isn't easy, the rewards are stupendous. The island is now the heart of a National Park covering 38 islands and a huge chunk of the Gulf of Chiriqui. Its ecological and marine importance is acknowledged by its designation (2005) as a UNESCO World Heritage Site. The Indo-Pacific current swirls its warmth through the Gulf and around Coiba, bringing with it coral, much of the Pacific tropical underwater life you just don't expect in the usually cold coastal waters of the Pacific Americas, and the larger fish/mammals like humpback whales, white tip, hammerhead, tiger and whale sharks, manta rays, barracuda, amberjack, big snappers, three kinds of marlin, and four kinds of sea turtle. The variety and numbers make for world-class diving – an obvious pedigree once you know that Coiba is the beginning of the underwater cordillera that includes both the Cocos Islands and the Galápagos.

**WHEN TO GO:**
January to April, the dry season, is the best time to see monkeys and onshore fauna; diving is superb year-round, but subject to unpredictable visibility.
**NEAREST TOWN:**
Santa Catalina is the closest access point for Coiba but Soná (about an hour away) has grocery stores, ATMs, etc.
**DON'T MISS:**
Barco Quebrado – where scarlet macaws gather in the largest concentrations on the planet, the most glamorous among Coiba's 150 amazing bird species. Diving off Bahia Damas, on Coiba's east side – the biggest – 135 hectares (334 acres) – coral reef in Central America.
The mantled howler monkeys, capuchins, fiddler and hermit crabs, Coiba agoutis, and boa constrictors and fer-de-lance on the Sendero de los Monos (Monkey Trail).
**YOU SHOULD KNOW:**
Because of the fragility of Coiba's ecosystem, and the necessity of knowing its waters well, diving and fishing trips should be arranged through local professionals. Local advice has it that 'anyone found tossing an anchor onto the reef will likely get an anchor tossed at his head'.

*A view of Coiba National Park, a group of volcanic islands located in the Panamanian Pacific*

**HOW TO GET THERE:**
There are several routes.
From Costa Rica: Bus from
San José to San Vito.
Or drive from San José to
San Isidro el General 153
km [92 mi]
From Panama: Fly or drive
to David, then an hour's
drive to Cerro Punta and
another 5km (3 mi) to Las
Nubes (Amistad
Administrative Centre).
Or fly to Changuinola then
an hour's drive to El
Silencio and boat trip to
Bocas del Toro (Amistad
Administrative Centre).

**WHEN TO GO:**
Caribbean side: hot and
wet all year. Pacific side:
dry season, December to
April. The temperature
varies according to altitude.

**NEAREST TOWN:**
Costa Rica: San Isidro el
General 25 km (15 mi);
Panama: Cerro Punta 5 km
(3 mi)

**YOU SHOULD KNOW:**
Much of the park has never
been explored and it would
be foolish to go very far
without a guide. The park
has entrance stations
(*puestos*) where you pay a
fee and pick up a map.
Camping is allowed at
Estacion Altimira and at
Estacion Las Tablas but
there is no lodging
anywhere in the park.
Much of the area is
2,000 m (6,560 ft) above
sea level so be prepared
for altitude.

# La Amistad National Park

La Amistad ("Friendship") is part of a cooperative Central American conservation project to create one continuous forest corridor from Mexico to Panama – an attempt to preserve the remains of a region in which 80 per cent of natural habitats have been destroyed.

The Park has a core zone of almost 6,000 sq km (2,300 sq mi) of pristine tropical rainforest in the ancient granite Cordillera de Talamanca – a vital watershed between the Pacific and Caribbean coasts containing the highest peaks of each country: Cerro Chirripó 3,819 m (12,526 ft) in Costa Rica, and Volcan Barú 3,475 m (11,398 ft) in Panama. The 25,000-year-old virgin rainforest is home to four Amerindian tribes – more than three quarters of Costa Rica's indigenous inhabitants.

There is an incredible diversity of species here, at the junction of North and South America. Tens of thousands of different kinds of plants flourish in the various life zones, which range from sea level mangrove habitats and lowland rainforest to montane forest and sub-alpine ecosystems. There is an area of virgin oak woodland containing seven species of oak

A *Hyla lancasteri* tree frog

(*Quercus*) and there are around 400 bird species and 260 sorts of reptile and amphibian. It is a habitat for Baird's tapirs, coatis, and howler, spider and capuchin monkeys as well as being one of the last refuges of the Central American wildcats – ocelot, tiger cat, jaguar and puma.

The Costa Rican side of the park is relatively inaccessible and only partially explored. There are no paved roads so you must travel on foot or horse. It is much easier to explore the park from the Panama side, but whichever route you choose, it is an amazing place for forest adventure, mountain hikes, riding, fishing and bird watching in many different environments of outstanding natural beauty.

# Exuma Cays

**WHAT IS IT?**
A coral island archipelago.
**HOW TO GET THERE:**
Fly from US or Nassau, or
ferry from Nassau to
Georgetown.
**WHEN TO GO:**
December to May, to avoid
the hurricane season.
**NEAREST TOWN:**
Georgetown.
**DON'T MISS:**
Iguanas on Allen's Cay –
one of the few places you
can still see these
prehistoric-looking but
harmless creatures.
Thunderball Cave on Staniel
Cay – this beautiful grotto
was a location in the film
*Thunderball*.

The Exuma Cays are a 150 km (90 mi) long chain of more than 360 cays and islands. Starting at Beacon Cay, 40 km (25mi) southeast of Nassau, they stretch southwards to the two main islands of the archipelago, Great Exuma and Little Exuma.

They are bounded on the west by the shallow waters and treacherous shifting sands of The Great Bahama Bank and on the east by the deep emerald green water of Exuma Sound, an undersea chasm whose sheer reef wall plummets hundreds of metres, with huge caverns and tunnels sheltering fish of all sorts and sizes. The Cays can only be explored by boat, which gives them a wonderful aura of remoteness and isolation even though they are only hours from civilization. They are sparsely populated, mainly by conch fishermen; the only sizeable settlement is Georgetown, on Great Exuma.

The Cays vary enormously in both size and terrain. Some are barely more than barren sandy chunks of reef; others are islands of densely vegetated rolling hills, with caves and grottos. Narrow channels of translucent aquamarine water, teeming with corals and tropical fish, run between them. The water visibility (25-45 m [80-145 ft]) and abundant marine life make them an outstanding place for diving and underwater photography.

The Exuma Cays Land and Sea Park, a no-fishing conservation area of 456 sq km (176 sq mi), contains 50,000 marine species. The Park is also a vital refuge for several rare iguana species, sea turtles, marine birds and an indigenous hutia. The Bahamas National Trust established the Park in 1959 with its headquarters on Warderick Wells Cay, 105 km (65 mi) southeast of Nassau. It is the oldest marine conservation park in the world.

*Following pages: An aerial view of the Exuma Cays*

*Abundant marine life and clear waters make the Exuma Cays an outstanding place for scuba diving.*

# Mariel to Valle de Viñales

**WHAT IS IT?**
Jurassic karst landscape.
**HOW TO GET THERE:**
Fly to Havana. Bus/taxi
from Havana 180 km
(112 mi)
**WHEN TO GO:**
Dry season: November
to April.
**NEAREST TOWN:**
Pinar del Rio 40 km (25 mi)
**DON'T MISS:**
Gran Caverna de Santo
Tomás, 16 km (10 mi) west
of Viñales – more than 46
km (29 mi) of underground
galleries and chambers full
of stalactites and
stalagmites, lakes
and rivers.
**YOU SHOULD KNOW:**
Don't attempt to hike
around here on your own;
people have been known to
disappear. The scenery is
deceptive and it is all too
easy to get lost and run out
of water.

Though relatively close to Havana, Cuba's far west has always been isolated from development or tourism by dense forests and rugged mountains. Its remote beauty has been made accessible by the extension of the Circuito Norte – the autopista that links Havana east and west along its north coast – to Pinar del Rio, and the paving of access roads close to some of the region's most breathtaking charms. Driving is certainly the most colourful way to see Cuba, and this is one of Cuba's very best scenic routes.

Once you clear the shabby suburbs of Havana, pure pleasure kicks in at Mariel, the fishing port once famous as the departure point for Cubans trying to reach Florida. With the sea sparkling on one side, you drive up into the green hills of the Sierra del Rosario, a protected UNESCO Biosphere Reserve of tropical mountain forests. Cut by numerous rivers and waterfalls, the Reserve is both stunningly beautiful and home to 100 bird species and more than half of Cuba's endemic species of flora and fauna. From the Circuito Norte it's easy to visit Las Terrazas, a woodland eco-community from which you can swim in the forest waterfalls and pools of the San Claudio Cascade, or the orchid gardens at Soroa.

It gets even better. The Valle de Viñales is a UNESCO World Heritage Site, designated as a

cultural landscape both for its astonishing beauty, and for its vernacular architecture and traditions. Dramatic panoramas feature huge rocky outcrops called *mogotes*, like islands towering out of a sea of green fields; and huge caves (once the refuge of remnant Taino Indians and runaway slaves) dot surrounding cliff faces. The Valley is Cuba's soul: it is wholly appropriate that such a lovely place is the only source of Cuba's finest tobacco leaves.

*The amazing karst scenery of the Viñales Valley*

# The Blue Mountains

The Blue Mountains are aptly named. They are enveloped in a permanent mist that, from a distance, suffuses them with a blue tint. They are renowned for their varied topography, biodiversity and staggering views, as well as the world's finest coffee, which is cultivated on the lower slopes.

The mountains rise from foothills at the north-eastern edge of the capital city of Kingston in a

steeply inclined escarpment over 2,000 m (7,000 ft) high that sweeps along eastern Jamaica for 48 km (28 mi). On a clear day, you can see Cuba from Blue Mountain Peak, the highest point in Jamaica at 2,256 m (7,402 ft). The heavily forested, rugged hinterland, 20 km (12 mi) deep, is scored with rapidly flowing rivers, streams and waterfalls, which cascade down into luxuriantly vegetated valleys causing frequent floods and landslides. More than 760 cm (300 in) of rain a year falls here, providing water for almost half Jamaica's population. The terrain is so wild that parts of it are still uncharted.

In the eighteenth century, the Maroons, fugitive slaves, set up their headquarters in the heart of this inaccessible mountainous jungle. They were so successful in waging guerrilla war against the British that eventually they were granted land rights. Today, their descendants, Rastafarian country farmers, conceal their ganja (marijuana) fields here.

There are more than 500 flowering plant species in the mountains, including the extraordinary Jamaica bamboo, *Chusquea abietifolia*, which flowers only once every 33 years. Over 200 species of resident and migrant bird thrive here, including hummingbirds (known locally as the "doctor bird"), and it is the home of the world's second largest butterfly, *Papilo homerus*.

In 1992 the Blue Mountain and John Crow National Park – with a total area of 780 sq km (255 sq mi) – was established to protect the remaining forest and watershed.

*A view across the staggering Blue Mountains*

**WHAT IS IT?**
Mountainous rainforest.
**HOW TO GET THERE:**
International airport, Montego Bay or Kingston then bus from Kingston.
**WHEN TO GO:**
Dry season: December to April. It is unwise to hike in the rainy season because of risk of landslides and floods.
**NEAREST TOWN:**
Kingston (less than an hour's drive)
**DON'T MISS:**
The numerous pools and waterfalls on the northern slopes.
**YOU SHOULD KNOW:**
It is not safe to hike on your own. Always use a guide in order to avoid getting into trouble by stumbling into illegal ganja fields or losing your way.

CARIBBEAN/JAMAICA

# Southern Reefs

Curaçao is a savannah island, outside the hurricane belt, off the coast of Venezuela. The largest of the Netherlands Antilles islands, it is renowned for spectacular reef diving as well as World Heritage colonial architecture and vibrant multi-culturalism.

The island is completely encircled by a fringe of coral reef, millions of years old. The northern coast is rocky with few beaches and strong ocean currents but the waters on the leeward (southern) side are wonderfully still. This 54 km (40 mi) long stretch of coastline, with its sheltered inlets and small sandy beaches nestling in rocky coves, has more than 80 superb diving sites, six of which are ranked among the best in the world.

Along the reef, known locally as the 'blue edge', the sea floor drops within exceptionally close range of the shore – less than 100 m (330 ft) away – making the southern reef one of the best places for shore diving in the whole of the Caribbean. Gentle slopes lead to dazzling coral walls, old shipwrecks and a myriad of marine life in calm, clear water with a visibility of over 30 m (100 ft). Massive outcrops of coral, teeming with tropical fish, extend to depths below 40 m (130 ft), which also makes for some fantastic wall and cave diving.

The Curaçao Underwater Park was established along 19 km (12.5 mi) of the southern coast in 1983 to protect the soft corals and sponges from the ravages of pollution and to ensure that the reef remains healthy and continues to sustain its present abundance of sea creatures.

**WHAT IS IT?**
A coral reef semi-desert island.

**HOW TO GET THERE:**
Direct flights from US and Amsterdam to Hato International Airport, 12 km (7 mi) northwest of Willemstad.

**WHEN TO GO:**
Any time. October to December are rainy months but, even then, showers are only ever moderate.

**NEAREST TOWN:**
Willemstad.

**DON'T MISS:**
Klein Curaçao – idyllic islet with sea turtles and dolphins. Hato Caves – unusual limestone formations, ancient Caiquetios Indian carvings and a colony of fruit bats.

**YOU SHOULD KNOW:**
Curaçao together with Bonaire and Aruba are known as the ABC islands. Curaçao has a murky past. In particular, Willemstad was at the hub of the slave trade and there are many historical traces of this to be seen in the culture and architecture.

*Following pages: The stunning Knip Beach*

*Row Pore Rope Sponge (Aplysina cauliformis)*

*A bromeliad in bloom just off the Mount Britton trail which winds through the El Yunque Rain Forest.*

# El Yunque

The Caribbean National Forest is the oldest nature reserve in the Western Hemisphere and is renowned for its primeval atmosphere and remarkable biodiversity.

Known as El Yunque, after the most important mountain in the Sierra de Luquillo, south east of San Juan, it is a relatively small subtropical rain forest, covering an area of 1,125 sq km (434 sq mi). The land was originally given protected status by King Alfonso

XII of Spain in 1876, his aim being to prevent his enemies taking wood from the forest for building boats. Today it is administered by the US Forest Service as part of the US National Forest System.

El Yunque is composed of four distinct vegetation types according to altitude: *tabonuco, palo colorado, palma sierra* and finally, at heights above 750 m (2,460 ft), the extraordinary dwarf or 'cloud forest, in which distorted trees, twisted into strange shapes by the wind, are shrouded in permanent mist.

A wide variety of plants thrive in the warm, wet environment. It rains almost every day, sometimes several times; in a year, the equivalent of 100 billion gallons of water flows down the mountainsides in cascading rivers and waterfalls. This abundance of water creates a benign habitat for over 240 tree and plant species, 26 of which are unique. There are 50 species of native orchid as well as tree vines, mosses, lichens, giant ferns and epiphytes. Rare wildlife includes the distinctive blue, green and red Puerto Rican parrot (*Amazonia vittata*), one of the ten most endangered species in the world, as well as the endangered Puerto Rican boa constrictor. The forest is also home to 13 species of *coqui* or tree frog, known for its distinctive sound, together with bats, lizards and 50 bird species.

**WHAT IS IT?**
A subtropical rainforest.
**HOW TO GET THERE:**
Scheduled international flights to San Juan.
**WHEN TO GO:**
All year. High season: December to April. Hurricane season: May to November (especially intense August to October).
**NEAREST TOWN:**
San Juan 40 km (25 mi)
**DON'T MISS:**
El Portal Rainforest Centre, Luquillo Beach.

# Islas Los Roques

**WHAT IS IS?**
The archipelago is one of the biggest national marine parks in the Caribbean.
**HOW TO GET THERE:**
By light aircraft from Caracas to El Gran Roque or by boat from Isla Margarita.
**WHEN TO GO:**
Year-round. Between July and September the possibility of storms muddying the water makes that period less suitable for scuba-diving.
**NEAREST TOWN:**
Caracas 130 km (80 mi), 40 minute flight.
**DON'T MISS:**
Sunset from the lighthouse (built 1870-80) on El Gran Roque – the archipelago dotted into the horizon, and on a clear day you can see Mt Avila (about 1,600 m, 5,000 ft) near Caracas. All the marvels to be seen and done on, in and under water next to one of the biggest and best coral reefs in the Caribbean.
**YOU SHOULD KNOW:**
There are no superlatives to describe the sense of peace you get in the Los Roques Archipelago.

The Los Roques Archipelago is one of the world's biggest National Marine Parks, and lies 145 km (80 mi) due north of La Guaira, the mainland port for Caracas. About 50 coral cays and sand bars are arranged in a huge oval around a lagoon, but it's only from the air you get a true idea of its scale – it covers the same area as the whole of the Virgin Islands.

The fragility of the islands and their ecosystem is all too obvious. Luckily they are shielded from eastern currents by a 24 km (15 mi) coral reef running from north to south, and a second barrier running 32 km (20 mi) from east to west. Protected since 1972, they represent a pristine environment that attracts only the most discerning visitors, who come either in their own boats or yachts in search of solitude and untrammelled tranquillity, or in small groups by light aircraft, often just for the day, from Caracas or elsewhere on the Venezuelan mainland. The island residents, who are descendants of the 110 families who originally came from Isla Margarita in the early 19th century, to make a living as fishermen, all live on El Gran Roque ('The Big Rock').

104

*Cayo de Agua*

They will welcome you as temporary family members, and you'll find that, along with the old style of manners and hospitality, they still use the old ways of fishing to catch lobsters, king conch and Spanish mackerel. If you're not staying on a boat, you'll probably eat the catch at one of the many *posadas* (small family lodges) scattered throughout the island, but all of which are within 100 m (328 ft) of the beach. Los Roques is about countless transmutations of blue and green beauty, and sharing the natural rhythms of a completely unspoiled, discrete ecosystem.

# Tayrona National Park

**WHAT IS IT?**
A gorgeous stretch of
unspoiled coastline.
**HOW TO GET THERE:**
By air from Bogota to
Santa Marta.
**WHEN TO GO:**
Rainfall is highest in May
and June and again from
September to November so
best to avoid these months.
**NEAREST TOWN:**
Santa Marta 34 km (21 mi)
**DON'T MISS:**
Diving in La Cueva de
Neguanje, Isla Aguja, or
Bahía Concha.
A trek to the archaeological
site of El Pueblito.
**YOU SHOULD KNOW:**
There are no hotels within
the park so camping or
Ecohabs are the only option.

North from Taganga, the Parque Nacional Tayrona
(Tayrona National Park) stretches for 85 km (53 mi), a
largely unspoiled and beautiful coastline where you can
see monkeys, iguanas and snakes in their natural habitat.
It covers 300 sq km (115 sq mi) of the Caribbean Sea and
1,200 sq km (460 sq mi) of coastline that rises to an
altitude of 975 km (3,200 ft) above sea level, affording
gorgeous views of the surrounding hillsides and pristine
beaches. Here the main objective is relaxation and
swimming in these azure protected waters. If you are
feeling inspired, you can always visit the archeological site
of Pueblito and its indigenous peoples.

Visitors to the park hike the scenic trails to the mouth
of the Piedras River, to the beautiful beaches of Cabo San

Juan de Guia, Arrecifes, Shell Bay or the Cove of Chengue.

The park is ideal for exploring and consists of a tropical dry forest, marine grass prairies and an exciting array of coral reefs with an abundance of undersea life. More than 100 species of land mammals and birds, from the common deer to the elusive white eagle, also call the park home.

Camping and ecotourism are the only options for overnight accommodation because here the importance of the conservation of the environment is taken very seriously. The ecohabs, or ecologically-friendly structures, are characteristic of the local Tayrona architecture, adding another element of charm to this already special place. If you prefer staying out of doors, El Cabo where you can hang your hammock and sway to the sea breezes, is one of the most popular campsites.

*Cabo San Juan de Guia beach*

*A Land iguana*

# Galápagos Islands

Ecuador's Galápagos Islands, a small archipelago straddling the Equator 965 km (600 mi) west of South America, are best known for being the site where Charles Darwin made the observations of the indigenous fauna that led him to develop his theory of evolution through natural selection. The group contains 13 main islands, six isles and 107 smaller rocks and islets, all of which are volcanic in origin.

On land, the land iguana and giant tortoises can be seen, and birds that nest here include masked, blue- and red-footed boobies, albatrosses, flightless cormorants, Galápagos flamingos, magnificent frigatebirds, Galápagos penguins and the buntings commonly called Darwin's finches. As well as an abundance of fish in the waters and among the reefs around the islands, the marine animals here include Galápagos sea lions, otters and marine iguanas.

Despite being a UNESCO World Heritage Site and marine reserve, these islands are under threat from a rapidly increasing population needing more resources, introduced species such as goats, cats and dogs and overfishing. The government of Ecuador has imposed strict controls on tourist access in order to prevent too many visitors destroying the very islands and wildlife that they come to see – a tour guide certified by the national park authority must accompany each group.

These spectacular but fragile islands, each with its own character, are a world treasure.

**WHAT IS IT?**
A stunning volcanic archipelago and one of the world's most important sites for conservation.
**HOW TO GET THERE:**
By air from Quito or Guayaquil
**WHEN TO GO:**
Any time of year.
**NEAREST TOWN:**
Guayalquil 1,000 km (620 mi)
**DON'T MISS:**
The colonies of nesting birds
**YOU SHOULD KNOW:**
Visitors to the islands must be accompanied by an accredited guide.

*Following pages:
Sea lions resting on
the sand along
Gardner Bay*

*A Giant Tortoise*

# Andes Cloud Forests

The mysterious cloud forests of Peru occur only at altitudes of 2,000-3,500 m (6,500 – 11,500 ft) on high mountains where the annual rainfall is 50-1,000cm (20-400in). The twisted, stunted trees with epiphytes and lichens trailing eerily from their branches are shrouded in perpetual mist. This is a unique ecosystem for thousands of species, 80 per cent of which are still undocumented. There are more than 1,000 species of orchid alone, and more than 30 per cent of the 272 endemic species of Peruvian mammals, birds and frogs live here.

The epithet 'Nature's water towers' applies with good reason: the forest is a vital source of pure water. The leaves of the trees and ferns draw moisture out of the clouds and drip it into the sodden peaty ground at a constant rate, contributing a regular controlled water supply to rivers lower down the mountains. The forest protects the watershed by preventing soil erosion as well as acting as a water collector. It is threatened by both climate change and man's encroachment, with potentially disastrous consequences for water supplies, quite apart from the loss of habitat for thousands of species of flora and fauna.

The huge 150,000 sq km (58,000 sq mi) World Heritage Site of Manú National Park was established to protect the remaining Peruvian cloud forest. Manú is a bird and wildlife watcher's utopia – a habitat for an incredible diversity of

**WHAT IS IT?**
A forest habitat for bird and wildlife watching
**HOW TO GET THERE:**
Fly to Lima then domestic flight or road to Cusco. 7 hours drive from Cusco to Paucartambo.
**WHEN TO GO:**
Any time but June to September is driest.
**NEAREST TOWN:**
Paucartambo 35 km (22 mi) from Ajunaco Pass, entrance to Manú National Park.
**YOU SHOULD KNOW:**
New species are being discovered all the time. The latest is a nocturnal rodent about the size of a squirrel (*Isothrix barbarabrownae*).

*A male Andean Cock-of-the-Rock*

species. Here you will see the Andean Cock-of-the-Rock – the bright scarlet national bird of Peru, the Mountain Toucan, quetzals, hummingbirds, and a myriad of butterflies unlike any you have ever seen. Amongst many other mammals, the Park is home to spectacled bears, woolly and brown capuchin monkeys, giant otters and jaguars.

This unique, romantic and fragile world makes up a mere 2.5 per cent of the tropical rainforest but its ecological significance is immeasurable.

*A Peruvian Yellow-tailed Woolly monkey*

# Central Amazon

The Amazon is the largest tropical rainforest in the world, a region of unparalleled diversity, with more than 150,000 species of plants 75,000 types of tree and 2,000 birds and mammals. Much of it is still unexplored – amazingly, we know less about the rainforest than we do about the ocean depths. 'The Lungs of the Planet' stretches across several nations and, in Brazil, 22,000 sq km (8,490 sq mi) has been

**WHAT IS IT?**
The largest tropical rainforest in the world.
**HOW TO GET THERE:**
International or domestic flights to Manaus.
**WHEN TO GO:**
Any time – hot and rainy all year.
**NEAREST TOWN:**
Manaus 16 km (10 mi) from Encontro das Aguas.
**DON'T MISS:**
The Black River Basin, the largest area of black water in the world, and the Carabinani Waterfalls, both in Jau National Park.
**YOU SHOULD KNOW:**
Amazonia produces 20 per cent of the earth's oxygen but is under serious threat. Of the 10 million or more indigenous people who once lived and worked in harmony with their surroundings, a mere 200,000 survive.

*A Yellow-Faced Amazon parrot*

115

set aside as the Jau National Park.

The usual route is by boat up the Rio Negro, whose black-coloured water is caused by decomposed organic matter and iron. It is the largest blackwater river in the world. The Rio Negro joins the muddy waters of the Amazon at the Encontro das Aguas ('Meeting of the Waters'). The pale waters of the Amazon and the dark ones of the Rio Negro flow side by side, in two distinct channels, for several kilometres. You will pass through dark, flooded *igapó*, in water up to 12 m (39 ft) deep – mysterious forest where strange epiphytes cling to the trees and the fauna has evolved complex survival strategies; *varsea* – a floating mosaic of vegetation, where the waters contain innumerable electric fish, the endangered manatee and the river dolphin; *terra firme*, above the water line – where, among huge tropical trees, you can pick up the trails of wild pig, jaguars and armadillos.

As you glide along this wide, slow river, past jungle shores of tangled vines under a magnificent green 45 m (148 ft) tall canopy, you cannot help being overwhelmed by a sense of the primitive forces that have shaped evolution. You will see plants of every conceivable shape and size, flashes of brilliant iridescent colours from butterflies and birds, and hear the sometimes spine-tingling calls of birds and animals echoing across the jungle. A trip into the Amazon rainforest is a truly life-transforming experience.

*Sailing down the Ariau
River at sunset*

# Emas National Park

**WHAT IS IT?**
Tropical savanna (Cerrado)
**HOW TO GET THERE:**
By road from Brasilia 700
km (440 mi) or Goiânia 500
km (312 mi) to Chapadão
do Céu.
**WHEN TO GO:**
April to October, to avoid
scorching heat.
**NEAREST TOWN:**
Chapadão do Céu 26 km
(16 mi)
**YOU SHOULD KNOW:**
Access is difficult so you
need to be determined.
There are no paved roads
in the area and you require
a permit to enter,
obtainable from the tourist
centre in Chapadão de Céu.

The remote Parc Nacional das Emas is a spectacular savanna plain (cerrado) of more than 1,300 sq km (500 sq mi) in central Brazil. Combined with the protected Cerrado of Chapada dos Veadeiros further north, it is a UNESCO Biosphere Reserve.

The granite plateau, ranging in altitude from 400-1,000 m (1,310 - 3,280 ft), is a magnificent Cerrado landscape – a vista of vast changing skies above rolling open-wooded grasslands. The plains are dotted with innumerable red earth termite mounds, scored with dramatic canyons and criss-crossed by rivers and clear rushing streams, with high waterfalls and black water drop pools.

The Park is part of the great dividing Cerrado plateau between the Amazon and Paraná River basins and is the site of the headwaters of the Araguaia, Formosa and Taquari rivers and their tributaries, which diverge across the plains making their separate ways to the Atlantic.

This is the place for hardcore nature lovers. Large mammals – troupes of monkeys, giant anteaters, tapirs, capybaras, armadillos, wild dogs, maned wolves, foxes, herds of deer, cougars and ocelots – roam freely here on a scale comparable with the savannas of East Africa, 87 species in all. It is also a birdwatcher's paradise, with more than 350 sorts of bird, including Aplomado falcons, Burrowing owls, Yellow-faced parrots and Macaws.

The termite mounds, which sprout surreally out of the ground, can be more than 2 m (6.6 ft) high. They are used as shelter by all sorts of wildlife including the larvae of the cumpinzeiro, a luminescent beetle. At night you may be fortunate enough to witness an extraordinary ephemeral display of nature when, after the rains, the landscape is transformed by the emergence of huge numbers of these insects. They light up the mounds in a fantastic display, transforming them into Christmas trees.

*Following pages:*
*A Collared anteater*

*The savanna at dawn*
*in Emas National Park*

118

# The Pantanal Wetlands

**WHAT IS IT?**
The world's largest freshwater wetlands.
**HOW TO GET THERE:**
Fly to Campo Grande or Cuiabá
**WHEN TO GO:**
Waters start to recede in April. Best from June to August
**NEAREST TOWN:**
Porto Jofre, Corumbá
**YOU SHOULD KNOW:**
The novel *The Testament* by John Grisham is largely set in the Pantanal.

The cattle ranching country of the Pantanal is the largest wetland area in the world. The diversity and abundance of vegetation and wildlife here is comparable to the Amazon and it is one of the most important eco-systems on the planet.

The Pantanal is a bowl-shaped depression covering a vast area of 250,000 sq km (96,500 sq mi) in central west Brazil, with two major river systems flowing through – Río Paraguay and Río Cuiabá. In effect, the region is a massive inland delta. In the rainy season the rivers burst their banks, flooding 80 per cent of the surrounding alluvial plain, providing nourishment for the world's largest collection of aquatic plants. These form floating islands of vegetation, *camalotes*, on which animals and birds take refuge from the water.

The region is habitat for 75 mammal species, among them the maned wolf, giant anteater, and the world's largest rodent, the capybara, weighing up to 60 kg, as well as five species of howler monkey, giant otters, peccaries, tapirs, deer and the occasional jaguar. There are over 300 species of fish, and Caiman alligators loll brazenly on the grassy river

banks. You will also see plenty of lizards, chameleons, land turtles, boa constrictors and anacondas. The region is a birdwatcher's paradise with more than 600 species – home to the jabiru, with its distinctive red crop, white plumage, black head and dark skinny legs, along with macaws, toucans, eagles, rheas and countless water birds.

It is a matter of great concern to conservationists that such a vital ecological region is largely unprotected, privately owned land used for ranching and eco-tourism. You can stay on one of these ranches and explore the marshes of the Pantanal by canoe or on horseback to catch sights of the superb wildlife, bird watch or go fishing.

*Following pages:*
*Pantanal Matogrossense*
*National Park*

*A toco toucan*
*(*Ramphastos toco*)*

# Fernando de Noronha

Calling the archipelago of 21 islands that includes Fernando de Noronha an idyllic paradise is an understatement. This area is one of the most important ecological sanctuaries in the world and in 2001, together with Rocas Atoll, it became a UNESCO World Heritage Site.

Seemingly abandoned amidst the clear blue waters of the Atlantic Ocean, the verdant mountains and sheer cliffs of Fernando de Noronha, a National Marine Reserve, jut out from the sea in all their lush, tropical glory. A beacon to divers from around the world, the waters surrounding the islands are home to a multitude of fish, manta rays, lemon sharks and spinner dolphins.

Every morning in the aptly named Baia dos Golfinhos (Bay of Dolphins), more than 1,000 spinner dolphins gather to frolic and dance in the early sunshine. Sea turtles are also prolific here, using many of the wide, secluded beaches as ground on which to lay their eggs.

The main island, Ilha de Fernando de Noronha, is the only one that is inhabited. To ensure the area's natural landscape is not damaged, only 420 guests can visit the island at any given time. The untouched land, 70 per cent of which is national parkland, is dotted by a limited number of sustainable tourist inns that are nearly always at full capacity, particularly in December and January.

The island has two distinct sides, a gentle coast facing Brazil and a rockier, rough coastline facing the Atlantic. The island is bisected by a single road running from Baia do Sueste to the eastern port of Baia Santo Antonio, close to Vila dos Remedios where the majority of the population resides. Here you will find the town hall, a church, the post office, a dive shop and a bar. Vila do Trinta, up a small hill, has a few restaurants, a pharmacy and a grocer.

The most impressive structure in town is the Forte dos Remedios, a crumbling reminder of the Portuguese occupation. Dating back to 1737, its ancient cannons are half buried, its ramparts on the edge of collapse. Down some cobbled streets you will also find a quaint yellow-and-white Baroque church, the Igreja Nossa Senhora dos Remedios, built in 1772, as well as the bright red colonial Palacio São Miguel.

The surrounding islands are largely characterized by their various formations. Meio Island, eroded to form a sort of inverted pyramid, is a well known landmark for sailors, its neighbour, Sela Gineta cliff, is also recognizable for its similarity in shape to a cowboy's saddle. Likewise, Chapéu do Sueste Island has been compared to a small mushroom and Ilha do Frade cliff has been said to resemble a bell, not only for its shape, but also for the sound of the waves striking against its rocky base. Morro do Leão cliff resembles a reclined sea lion, and the two imposing dark volcanic islands of Dois Irmãos cliff are said to resemble a woman's breasts.

Whatever you see in the cliffs, the image of a tropical paradise is the one that will remain with you forever.

*Cacimba do Padre beach*

*A view across the rainforest in the Noel Kempff Mercado National Park*

# Noel Kempff Mercado National Park

This exceptional biological reserve, named after a renowned Bolivian biologist, is a truly awe-inspiring region of more than 15,000 sq km (5,790 sq mi) of remote wilderness in northeast Bolivia. It is one of the least disturbed expanses of land in the Amazon basin, and one of the most biologically diverse areas in the world. The scenery is breathtaking – extraordinary landscapes, vast rivers, and stunning waterfalls.

A visit to the Park is a fantastic eco-adventure. The sheer scale of the wilderness Cerrado (the largest remaining virgin tract of this rich savanna land in the world) is staggering – broad rivers cut through the savanna, their banks lined with strangely contorted trees, and great cascades of water thunder down into the streams and creeks of the rainforest. The terrain ranges in altitude from 200-1,000 m (655-3,280 ft) and encompasses five distinct eco-systems. It is a refuge for wildlife that has largely disappeared from the rest of the Amazon. There are more than 130 species of mammal here, including rare river otters, river dolphins, spider and howler monkeys, maned wolves, giant armadillos and an endangered population of black jaguars. So far, biologists have documented around 4,000 species of flora, 110 species of orchid alone, as well as at least 620 sorts of bird and 70 kinds of reptile, some of the world's rarest insects and an incredible population of butterflies, of all colours and sizes.

The park dates back over a billion years, to the Pre-Cambrian period. Its remoteness and diversity make it an ideal laboratory for biological research into the evolution of ecosystems. Nowhere else in South America can you see such a wide variety of species and habitats with so little effort.

**WHAT IS IT?**
A diverse wilderness, designated by UNESCO as 'Natural Patrimony of Humanity'.

**HOW TO GET THERE:**
Fly to Santa Cruz. Fly or drive 600 km (375 mi) from Santa Cruz to Flor de Oro or Los Fierros Park lodges.

**WHEN TO GO:**
The ideal season is October to December.

**DON'T MISS:**
The awe inspiring Caparú Plateau – a Pre-Cambrian sandstone *mesa* (table mountain), rising straight up from the rainforest, one of the places that lays claim to being the inspiration for Sir Arthur Conan Doyle's story *The Lost World*.

**YOU SHOULD KNOW:**
There are very few visitors because of the park's remoteness. You approach the park from either the north or south depending upon where you have pre-arranged your stay – Flor de Oro (north) or Los Fierros (south).

# Lauca World Biosphere Reserve

**WHAT IS IT?**
A beautiful region of mountains and highlands.
**HOW TO GET THERE:**
International airports Santiago or Iquique, then domestic flight to Arica 145 km (91 mi) from the park and road to Putre.
**WHEN TO GO:**
Anytime. Extreme high altitude desert climate with a sharp drop in temperature to below 0 ºC (32ºF) at night.
**NEAREST TOWN:**
Putre 12 km (7.5 mi)

Lauca is in the Altiplano – the most extensive area of high plateau in the world outside Tibet, and one of the most beautiful regions of Chile. It is a protected area of almost 3,600 sq km (1,390 sq mi) along the border with Bolivia, designated a UNESCO World Biosphere Reserve.

More than 3,000 m (9,840 ft) above sea level, the Altiplano separates the Atacama Desert from the Amazon Basin. It is homeland to a dwindling number of llama and alpaca herdsmen – the remnants of a pastoral society of Aymará Indians whose culture is rich in a tradition of music and festivals. There are many archaeological sites and geoglyphs, attesting to a civilization that goes back thousands of years.

The terrain is gashed by deep gorges with fast flowing rivers and streams, dotted with lagoons, lava

outcrops, brackish marshes and sparkling saltpans, with a stunning backcloth of active and dormant volcanoes. It sustains three distinct sorts of plant life: shrubs and cacti; perennial grass, *paja brava* – used for thatch; *llareta*, a pungent cushion plant, which only grows 1 mm (0.004 in) per year, traditionally used as medicine and for fuel. Around 130 bird species, including Andean gulls and condors, and 21 kinds of mammal live here. In Salar de Surire, an extensive salt marsh, there are numerous rare plants and animals, including three species of flamingo.

One of the most beautiful places in Lauca is Lago Chungará, an emerald coloured lake formed 8,000 years ago when a major eruption caused 6 cu km (1.5 cu mi) of volcanic debris to avalanche. Whether or not Lago Chungará is the world's highest lake at 4,500 m (14,760 ft), as the locals claim, it is a spectacular place to visit for the hundreds of unusual birds and incredible views of the Payachatas volcanoes, with their perfectly symmetrical snowy-tipped cones.

**DON'T MISS:**
The Cotacotani lagoons, connected by channels and cascades.
**YOU SHOULD KNOW:**
Very high elevations so you must give yourself time to acclimatize in order to avoid altitude sickness.

*Mount Parinacota seen from Lago Chungará*

# Torres del Paine

Mention the words Torres del Paine to a serious walker and the chances are you will be met with an expression of awed reverie. This national park in the far south of Chile has long been a legendary destination among the trekking community and the eponymous 'Towers' – a cluster of 2,600-m (8,530-ft) granite pillars that make up the Paine Massif at the heart of the park – have become the defining image of Patagonia in many people's minds. There are enough different aspects of elemental nature here to satisfy the most seasoned of travellers: rugged mountain terrain, thundering rivers in deep-sided valleys, wide-open steppes and dense green forests. And being so far south you find a magical extra ingredient in the mix: huge glaciers and lakes with floating chunks of shimmering blue ice the size of a house. The most accessible is the Grey glacier and its associated lake (which is anything but that colour), although it is still a long day's hike to the base of the glacier.

The breathtaking scenery in this national park fully deserves its reputation but it does mean that it is a popular place and can get very busy with hikers in the summer months. Most walkers come to tackle the

'W', one of the world's classic treks, so called because of the route's shape on the map. The 'W' takes four to five days to complete and there are good campsites and mountain shelters throughout the park. The route includes a number of fantastic viewpoints (*miradores*) and the Valle Francés, a steep-sided valley with spectacular mountain views on both sides. If you have the time and the stamina, the Circuit Trail (seven to ten days) takes you round the back of the peaks and gets you away from the crowds.

*The steep granite towers known as* cuernos *(horns) tower above emerald Lake Pehoe*

133

# Los Glaciares

**WHAT IS IT?**
Glaciers!
**HOW TO GET THERE:**
Fly to El Calafate
International airport or by
road from Río Gallegos.
**WHEN TO GO:**
October to April. High
season January and
February.
**NEAREST TOWN:**
El Calafate 40km (25 mi)
**DON'T MISS:**
The Walichu Caves; La
Leona Petrified Forest. Only
one day away, on the other
side of the border in Chile,
is the Torres del Paine
Biosphere Reserve.

The World Heritage Site of Los Glaciares National Park is a region of awe-inspiring beauty in the Southern Patagonian Ice Field – the third largest continental icecap in the world after Antarctica and Greenland. Los Glaciares extends 170 km (106 mi) along the Chilean border, more than a third of it covered in ice. It is 4,450 sq km (1,720 sq mi) of arid steppe, wondrous coloured beech forests, glacial lakes and the towering mountains of the Andean ice cap.

The ice cap is the direct source of 47 large glaciers and there are around 200 smaller unconnected ones. Glaciers normally occur at altitudes of 2,500 m (8,200 ft) or more. Here, uniquely, they are only 1,500m (4,920 ft) above sea level, so are easily accessible.

The park has two huge lakes – the 160 km (100 mi) long Lake Argentino in the south and Lake Viedma in the north – around which you can explore some of the most extreme scenery in the world.

Lake Viedma is dominated by the awesome granite spikes of the FitzRoy Massif, great jagged walls of rock towering up out of the forest. Otherwise known as Cerro Chaltén (Smoking Mountain) because of the ring of cloud round its peak, Mount FitzRoy has the reputation of being 'ultimate', not because it is particularly high at 3,375 m (11,070 ft) but because of its sheer granite sides.

At one end of Lake Argentino is the incredible spectacle of continual ice-falls. It is the junction of three glaciers – The Onelli, the Upsala and Spegazzini. Together with the immense 5 km (3 mi) wide Perito Moreno glacier, they make their inexorable descent from the ice cap, eroding the mountain in their path, to disgorge colossal icebergs into the milky waters of the lake in an overwhelming display of nature's power.

*Following pages:*
*Perito Moreno Glacier*

*The Upsala glacier*

# EUROPE

# Aurora Borealis

**WHAT IS IT?**
An electric display of atmospheric fireworks.
**HOW TO GET THERE:**
To see the aurora borealis in Iceland you must fly to Reykjavik.
**WHEN TO GO:**
The best months are October to March, late autumn being the best time of all.
**NEAREST TOWN:**
Get as far away from town and its light pollution as possible.
**DON'T MISS:**
Haukadalur Valley, 193 km (120 mi) north of Reykjavik, the home of the Great Geysir.
**YOU SHOULD KNOW:**
Aurora 'forecasts' can be found on the internet, search for 'spaceweather'. For much of the summer the Icelandic sky never really gets dark enough to see the aurora.

The aurora borealis is Nature's very own lightshow, a shimmering stream of coloured light that suffuses the night sky. Visually stunning, part of an aurora's beauty lies in its ephemeral nature. You can never be sure when you will see one and you can never be sure what kind of display you will witness. Sometimes an aurora can be a disappointingly monochrome, diaphanous cloud. At others a pulsating psychedelic curtain of colours.

This remarkably sci-fi phenomenon has an equally remarkable sci-fi explanation. It occurs when electrically charged particles, travelling at speeds of up to 1,200 km (750 mi) per second on the solar wind, are captured by the earth's magnetic field. As these particles are drawn down towards the poles they hit the ionosphere and collide with the gases in the atmosphere. These collisions produce photons – light particles that glow red, green, blue and violet. The result is a shimmering sky show known as the aurora australis in the southern hemisphere and the aurora borealis, or northern lights, in the north.

Auroras appear over the poles in what are described as auroral ovals. These ovals dip further south when the solar winds are stronger, but most auroras are seen at latitudes higher than 65°N – which includes all of Iceland.

Viewing is best on crisp clear evenings in late autumn and winter, away from the glare of city lights, when the nights are long and dark. Although visually spectacular, the light of an aurora is dimmer than starlight – so if you cannot see any stars you are unlikely to see the northern lights.

*The incredible northern lights shimmer over the Reykjanes Peninsula.*

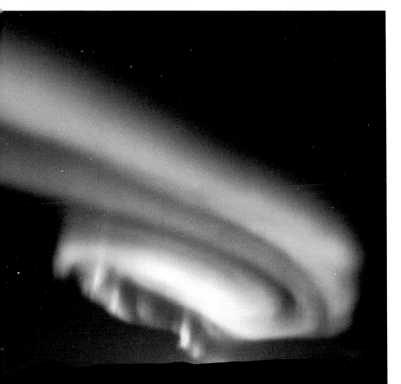

*Maelifell volcano rises from a desert of laval ash.*

# Maelifell

In a country full of remarkable volcanic creations, one of the more unusual is Maelifell. It's an unnaturally uniform cone that rises from a barren desert of laval ash. It was created by an eruption under the Myrdalsjökull glacier in southern Iceland. Its cone is made up of 'tuff', a mixture of solidified ash and other volcanic debris, and rises some 200 m (650 ft) above the plain.

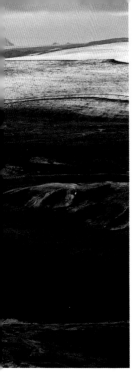

About 10,000 years ago Myrdalsjökull, Iceland's most southerly, and fourth largest, glacier, finally loosened its icy grip on Maelifell, exposing this pointy little peak to the Icelandic sun. As a consequence, this mysterious cone became clothed in a soft coat of moss. The moss, grimmia, is one of the 500 kinds of moss that make up a large percentage of Iceland's rather uninspiring 1,300 plant species. Grimmia thrives on laval soils, but what is most remarkable about it is its colour. Where the soil is dry it grows a somewhat inconspicuous silver-grey colour. But where the soils are moist, as they are on Maelifell, grimmia turns a bright, almost luminous green.

Surrounded by the dusty Maelifellsandur Desert, Maelifell's feet are washed by the numerous braided rivers and streams that flow from Myrdalsjökull. It's a quite otherworldly landscape presided over by the silent green cone of Maelifell.

Maelifell hasn't erupted for over 10,000 years, long enough for even the most conservative volcanologist to confidently consider it extinct. But a little further south, still underneath the ice of Myrdalsjökull, lies Katla, one of the most active volcanoes in Iceland. Katla last erupted in 1918 and experts believe that another eruption could occur very soon.

**WHAT IS IT?**
A volcanic cone.
**HOW TO GET THERE:**
The bus to Kirkjubaejarklaustur from Reykjavik takes 5 hours.
**WHEN TO GO:**
Spring to autumn.
**NEAREST TOWN:**
Kirkjubaejarklaustur
**DON'T MISS:**
The 62 m (200 ft) high waterfall Skogafoss at Skogar.
**YOU SHOULD KNOW:**
Maelifell can only be reached either on foot or by 4 wheel drive.

# Geirangerfjord

The Geirangerfjord is considered the archetype of fjords – the most scenically beautiful fjord of all in a fairytale region of sublime natural beauty. Geiranger is part of the intricate Norwegian fjord system that stretches from Stavanger in the south 500 km (300 mi) northwards along the western coast. The terrain here has been shaped by glaciation to create some of the most outstanding scenery in the world.

Geirangerfjord is a 15 km (9 mi) long stretch of deep blue water, branching off from the Storfjord in a narrow, winding ravine of hairpin bends and sheer crystalline rock escarpments. The cliff face is up to 1,400 m (4,600 ft) high and plunges 500 m (1,640 ft) below sea level. A series of spectacular waterfalls cascade down the sides of the ravine. The most famous are the Seven Sisters and the Suitor, facing each other on opposite sides of the fjord, and the Bride's Veil, so called because, when backlit by the sun, it gives the impression of a thin veil trailing over the rocks.

The surrounding scenery is breathtaking – a landscape of rugged, ice-capped mountains, glacial lakes, and deciduous and coniferous forests traversed by rivers. Along the sides of the fjord, you will see many abandoned smallholdings – historic traces of the way the people of this region scratched a living from the soil before the days of mass tourism. These ramshackle dwellings are in isolated shelves of land along the escarpments; some of them are surrounded by such steep slopes that they can only be accessed by ladder from a boat. When the farmers wanted to avoid the taxman, they simply drew up their ladders and relied on nature to protect them from the authorities.

*Right: The Seven Sisters waterfalls*

*Following pages: A view of the eastern end of Geirangerfjord*

145

# Lofoten Islands

West of mainland Norway, the Lofoten Islands lie more than 67° north of the equator, within the Arctic Circle. Despite this, they have a relatively mild climate because of the warm waters of the Gulf Stream.

There are five main islands – Austvågøy, Gimsøya, Vestvågøy, Flakstadøya and Moskenesøya – and three smaller ones – Vaerøy, Røst and the tiny islet of Vedøy. They are mountainous, with wooded hillsides and are fringed with pretty bays and beautiful white, sandy beaches.

The islands are surrounded by rich waters that support vast colonies of breeding seabirds, including puffins, kittiwakes, razorbills, red-necked phalaropes

*Twilight over the Lofotens*

and Arctic terns, as well as white-tailed sea eagles. Rare birds like capercaillie and black grouse can sometimes be spotted. In summer, sperm whales can be found offshore, while orca follow the herring to this area in early autumn. Seals and otters can also be seen and there are moose on Austvågøy.

One of the biggest deep-water coral reefs, the 40-km (25-mi) long Røst Reef is just west of Austvågøy and off the coast of Moskenesøya lies the vast whirlpool, the Maelstrom.

The spectacular ruggedness of these islands makes them popular with climbers and hikers, and the beautiful coastline is a favourite destination for cyclists. In midsummer, this beautiful area becomes even more magical, as for more than seven weeks, the sun remains above the horizon.

*The picturesque village of Reine*

*The Rapa River delta*

# Sarek National Park

The World Heritage Site of Laponia is known more prosaically as Sweden's northernmost province of Norrbotten, and it is the ancestral home of the nomadic Sami reindeer herders. It is a harsh, remote world, far above the Arctic Circle, of glacial lakes and valley wetlands, alpine massifs, ravines, rivers and

spectacular mountain peaks rising above glittering icefields and glaciers. Most of it is a trackless wilderness, protected by a series of national parks that border Norway to the west, and stretch almost to Finland in the east. Each park has a signature terrain, but their common heart is Sarek, where Sweden's greatest concentration of high peaks sits in icy majesty. Of some 250 distinct mountains, 87 are over 1,800 m (5,900 ft) and eight soar over 2,000 m (6,560 ft), packed into a rough circle spanning 50 km (31 mi). Although the park contains nearly 100 glaciers, it suffers a lot of rain which can turn streams into torrents without warning. In fact, crossing rivers is a major hazard in Sarek, where two bridges over key trail junctions are the only facilities available to help hikers. The bridge over the Smaila River at the park's centre is all-important, and visitors use it as both destination and meeting point. From the outside it takes two to three days to reach – from Rinim through the Pastavagge; from Kisuris through the Ruotesvagge; or, most magically of all, from Aktse along Rapadalen.

Rapadalen is Sarek's main artery. Fed by the waters of 30 glaciers, the Rapapaato River flows like threads, braided and spread across the broad valley floor, settling in ponds and small lakes. The water is coloured a bright, ice green against the emerald shrubs on its soggy banks, and fingers of mist shroud nearby mountain tops and hover in side canyons. It's one of Europe's most beautiful places, and worth making every effort to see.

**WHAT IS IT?**
A spectacular World Heritage Site home to 100 glaciers and six of Sweden's highest peaks.

**HOW TO GET THERE:**
By car or bus from Jokkmokk to Ritsem, then by Lapp boat across Lake Akkajaure; or on foot via the Kungsleden or Padjelanta marked trails through adjoining national parks.

**WHEN TO GO:**
Any time. The northern lights are usually at their best between November and February.

**NEAREST TOWN:**
Kiruna 150 km

**DON'T MISS:**
Laddepakte, Skarjatjakka and Skierfe are easily accessible mountain peaks, with some of the best panoramas over Sarek. Look out for the bizarrely exuberant herbaceous flora of Rapadalen, and dense stands of mountain birch and osier that encourage the presence of bear, arctic fox, lynx, wolverine and the large elk of the region.

**YOU SHOULD KNOW:**
Sarek National Park is not for the inexperienced. Professional polar explorers come here to train, and so do climbers practising for major assaults. Some of the hiking is fairly easy (especially in summer, although the downside is zillions of swarms of mosquitoes), but beginners can be caught out by conditions changing from benign to treacherous in seconds.

*Following pages: A view across Rapadalen*

153

# Lake Inari

**WHAT IS IT?**
The largest lake in Lapland.
**HOW TO GET THERE:**
The nearest airport is in Ivalo. Inari is over 15 hours by bus from Helsinki.
**WHEN TO GO:**
May to July for the Midnight Sun. The lake is frozen from November to June.
**NEAREST TOWN:**
Ivalo, 45 km (28 mi) south.
**DON'T MISS:**
The Inari Sámi Museum, devoted to the culture of the indigenous Sámi people. In addition to the indoor exhibition, there is an outdoor museum featuring traditional Sámi dwellings.

Situated on the 69th parallel, deep inside the Arctic Circle, lies Finland's third largest lake – Lake Inari. The sixth largest in Europe, Lake Inari is actually more like a small sea. Measuring around 1,000 sq km (386 sq mi), by the time you have sailed out to its often choppy centre, the shore will have long disappeared. Almost completely frozen for more than half the year, the last of the winter ice usually melts away by the second week of June. But even on the warmest days the water temperature only just makes it into double figures.

The Finnish name for Finland, Suomi, means 'land of lakes' – Lake Inari is, by contrast, a 'lake of lands' with over 3,000 islands peppering its surface and providing a fascinating water-borne tableau for visitors to explore.

Cruises are a popular way to enjoy the lake – although for the more adventurous all manner of watercraft, from small motorboats to kayaks, are

*The Midnight Sun over Lake Inari*

available for hire. Around the lake's 2,776 km (1,725 mi) rocky and rugged shoreline there are numerous discoveries to make.

At Ukonkivi there is an old sacrificial site that the Sámi people used to ensure good fishing. And when their catches were good they would store the surplus in ice caves such as the one on Iso-Maura that stays frozen all year. Fish remain one of the lake's more

*A view across a misty Lake Inari*

abundant resources, with whitefish, trout and Arctic char the most common species. More obvious are the mergansers and red-throated divers that come here to fish and whose hauntingly strange calls float across the water.

Visitors in summer can enjoy the delights of Lake Inari by day or night as from May to the end of July the sun never completely sets. The temperature at this time can reach a warmish 13 °C (55 °F). But it doesn't last long. And then when the ice freezes in November the lake is plunged into the one-and-a-half-month-long *Kaamos*, or dark season.

# Berchtesgaden Alps

Berchtesgaden National Park, in the far south-east of Bavaria and on the border with Austria, is the only alpine national park in Germany and is popular with walkers, hikers and climbers. Within it lie the Watzmann massif, the third highest mountain in the country, and the Königssee, a beautiful glacial lake. The slopes of the glacial valleys are carpeted with dense forest, separated by deep gorges while the valley bottoms make an idyllic farmland.

As its name suggests, the Königssee (King's Lake) was popular with the Bavarian royal family, and it is still a popular place for recreation today. It remains peaceful because the only powered boats allowed on it are electric: its water is reputed to be the cleanest in Germany. Its 5.2 sq km (2 sq mi) of beautiful clear waters reflect the mountains that surround it on all sides and canoeing is a favourite activity here. Looming over the lake is the Watzmann

**WHAT IS IT?**
A mountainous region in the south-east of Bavaria.
**HOW TO GET THERE:**
By road from Munich.
**WHEN TO GO:**
Summer.
**NEAREST TOWN:**
Berchtesgaden 5 km (3 mi)
**DON'T MISS:**
The view from the top of the Kehlstein.
**YOU SHOULD KNOW:**
The Watzmann is a very tough climb, and should be undertaken only by climbers who have achieved the necessary levels of expertise.

*A meadow in bloom in the Berchtesgaden Alps*

massif, a popular challenge reserved for experienced climbers only.

The National Park, which covers 210 sq km (81 sq mi) was declared a UNESCO Biosphere Reserve in 1990 because of its alpine landscape and its wildlife, which includes griffon vulture, bearded vulture,

golden eagle, chamois, red fox and roe deer.

A popular hike for many is up the 1,835-m (6,020-ft) Kehlstein. Most famous as the site of Hitler's command complex and the Eagle's Nest retreat, the top of this peak provides stunning views across the valley.

*Mount Watzmann towers over the town of Berchtesgaden.*

# Rügen

*Stunning white cliffs in
Jasmund National Park*

It's only 51 km (32 mi) long and 43 km (27 mi) at its
widest, but Rügen, the Baltic island close to
Germany's northeast border with Poland, has an
astonishing 574 km (357 mi) of coastline. Inevitably,
the long strands of white sand backed by ancient
woodlands and gleaming lakes have made Rügen one
of Germany's most popular holiday resorts for
generations of visitors. Much more remarkable is that
the island has preserved its greatest natural treasures
intact. Nature parks protect three distinct – and rare
– aspects of the Baltic coastline; and guard the
pastoral idyll of Rügen's interior against over-
enthusiastic development.

Biggest (22,500 hectares) and most important is
the Biosphere Reserve of Southeast Rügen, a region
of peninsulas, small islands, hooked spits, and sand
bars barely submerged beneath shallow, inland
waters. It includes the Granitz forest, the Monchgut

peninsula and Vilm, a
small island whose oak
and beech forest has
remained untouched for
whole centuries, and
whose unique delights
can only be visited by
appointment. Hiddensee,
a long, thin island within
the West-Pomeranian
Boddenschaft Reserve at
the other side of Rügen,
shares a similar landscape
of dunes, forests, salt
marshes, and lagoons of
brackish water typical of
the Baltic. The ratio of
salt to fresh water makes

*Wildflowers on Rügen*

these 'Bodden' invaluable habitats to millions of
migratory birds. Every autumn, around 30,000 cranes
arrive in one of Europe's most dramatic avian
spectacles. Cars are forbidden on Hiddensee, and
its isolated wetlands are a habitat for some of the
rarest flora and fauna in the world. Here, earth and
water merge under the piercing clarity of huge,
northern skies.

One of Rügen's loveliest walks takes you through
the Jasmund Reserve on the east coast. The
Königsstuhl (King's Chair) is the highest point of
Germany's only pure white, chalk cliffs. At 10 km
(6 mi) long and up to 117 m (384 ft) high, the cliffs
illustrate the dynamics of coastal erosion – and there's
a visitor centre of exceptional interest and quality
that helps explain this and the other features that
make Rügen so special.

# The Spreewald

Just 100 km (62 mi) south of Berlin is a huge nature reserve 75 km (47 mi) long and 15 km (9 mi) wide. It is a lowland of water meadows and broadleaf woods that developed 20,000 years ago during the Ice Age, intersected by 970 km (606 mi) of streams and water courses, and is unique in central Europe. Incredibly, so close to Germany's capital, it has resisted history: its people, the Sorbs, one of only two recognized minorities with their own ancient customs, dress and still-spoken language, and its landscape have both remained intact and untouched. The Spreewald is a paradise of benign wilderness given over to thousands of very rare species of plants and animals.

However you reach the Spreewald region, you need a boat to travel within it. There are thousands of waterways (called *Fliesse*), broad and narrow, and punts are the usual transport for local farmers as well as visitors. Motor boats are discouraged because they are noisy – and the Spreewald demands maximum attention from all the senses. You hear, touch and smell the rushes bowing on the breeze, the gurgle of water and creaking wood of the punt, overlaid with the snap of wings as storks, hoopoes, cranes and curlews lift off in sudden, flapping urgency. The more you listen, the more the watery stillness comes alive with the sound of living things. Thousands of butterflies dart in the leafy canopy of

poplars, oak trees and the slender alders that dapple the sunlight over the streams. Fish leap; dragonflies dart and hum; birds sing their glory. Lilies float companionably, and wild flowers dot every leafy corner of the marshy labyrinth.

Take a canoe or a kayak, or hire a punt (perhaps with a guide to identify the flora and fauna), or ride a bicycle, or stroll, or hike. There's no public transport. The Spreewald succeeds in being remote even in the middle of an industrialized society.

*One of the thousands of waterways (Fliesse) that flow through the broadleaf woods of the Spreewald.*

**WHAT IS IT?**
A forest Biosphere Reserve with a unique no-intervention policy.
**HOW TO GET THERE:**
By car/train (the 'Waldbahn') to Zwiesel, Eisenstein, Grafenau or Frauenau; then by bus.
**WHEN TO GO:**
Year-round.
**NEAREST TOWN:**
Eisenstein/ Neuschonau (N), Grafenau (S).
**DON'T MISS:**
The 7 km (4.4 mi) loop through the wilderness enclosure where the Lynx Project is flourishing.
**YOU SHOULD KNOW:**
The spruce bark beetle is under 6 mm (1/5 in) long. Just 50 can kill a fully-grown tree in 8 weeks.

*Snow-covered trees in Germany's oldest national park*

# Bayerische Wald

The oldest of Germany's national parks, the Bayerische Wald winds around the Bavarian forest peaks of Falkenstein, Rachel and Lusen along the border with the Czech Republic. In partnership with the neighbouring Sumava National Park in the Czech Republic, it is the largest protected forest area in central Europe. Nowhere else between the Atlantic Ocean and the Ural mountains has a major forest been returned completely to nature. No human lives there; and no human intervention is allowed to shape the development of the forest in any way. With no agriculture, husbandry or commercial logging, the forest has regenerated a wide variety of habitats among its many wet valleys, streams, bogs, moors and meadows. Rare species like the lynx, black stork, eagle owl, pygmy owl, three-toed woodpecker, and Bohemian gentian have returned, among hundreds of others. In some places, huge tracts of spruce lie in

rotting tumbles, shrouded in moss and undergrowth: your heart sinks until you see the evidence of a whole new kind of forest emerging from centuries of commercial exploitation which have left it vulnerable to the ravages of the bark beetle, agent of the devastation. As the bark beetle kills off the spruce, nature is replacing them with the truly native beech, mountain ash, rowan and other deciduous species, which in turn are attracting even greater varieties of flora and fauna.

*A rare lynx in Bayerische Wald*

You can witness this unique landscape along 300 km (187 mi) of walking trails and 200 km (125 mi) of cycling paths. The Hochwaldsteig takes you (via Jacob's ladder) to the 1,373 m (4,503 ft) rock dome of the Lusen, above the tree line; the Watzlikhain, near the Zwieslerwaldhaus sanctuary, is a forest wilderness discovery path; and the Igelbus (the national park bus) will drop you at the Seelensteig, a trail of such contemplative beauty that will crush your inner demons. But when you come to Bayerische Wald for the first time, visit the information centre at Neuschonau for one-to-one advice on how best to enjoy your personal enthusiasms, and a first-class children's discovery room.

# The Camargue

**WHAT IS IT?**
A vast area of marshland.
**HOW TO GET THERE:**
By road from Arles.
**WHEN TO GO:**
Late spring to early
autumn.
**NEAREST TOWN:**
Arles 5 km (3 mi)
**DON'T MISS:**
The flamingos on the
Étang Fangassier.
**YOU SHOULD KNOW:**
Bring mosquito repellant.

A vast, beautiful expanse of wild marshland and
lagoons on the Mediterranean's Golfe du Lion, the
Camargue is a protected area full of wildlife. It is
formed by silt deposited by the Grande and Petit
Rhône rivers as they reach the sea and is continually
encroaching into the Mediterranean. The northern
part and the edges were turned over to agriculture,
primarily red Camarguais rice, in the middle of the
twentieth century, but
the central part,
sheltered from the sea
by sand bars, remains
as a haven for wildlife.
The Étang de Vaccarès
was declared a regional
park in 1927 and was
incorporated into the
Parc Régional de
Camargue in 1972.

The Camargue
covers an area of 930 sq
km (360 sq mi). The
briny lagoons (*étangs*)
and reed marshes are
home to thousands of
birds and also provide a
haven for migrants,
with a total of more
than 400 species of
birds having been
recorded here. The
symbol of the area is
the greater flamingo, of
which some 13,000
breed on the Étang
Fangassier. Mammals in

*A Greater flamingo
colony on the Étang
Fangassier*

the area include badgers, beavers and wild boar.

The other animals for which the area is famous are the white horses and the black bulls. The bulls roam free, guarded by *gardiens*, who ride tamed Camarguais horses.

The area has been exploited by humans for thousands of years, for agriculture and for extracting salt and some of the dykes created for water-control purposes give access to the inner marsh. It is also possible to explore by canoe or you can hire a horse.

*Following pages:*
*Camarguais horses*

# Les Gorges du Verdon

The second largest canyon on earth, after the Grand Canyon, Les Gorges du Verdon are a spectacular sight in the north of Provence. Known only to the locals until 1905, the gorge was 'discovered' by the caver Edouard Alfred Martel and rapidly became a tourist attraction. Its proximity to the Provençal coast made it an ideal place to retreat during the heat of summer. Millions of years ago, this area was under a forerunner of the Mediterranean Sea and layer upon layer of limestone and then coral were deposited over the whole area. After the region was lifted up because of the northwards movement of Africa, the

*A view over Les Gorges du Verdon*

land was crumpled and cracked, allowing water and ice to find their way through faults in the soft rock, creating caverns and underground rivers, whose ceilings finally collapsed, slowly etching out this deep, v-shaped valley.

The gorge is only about 20 km (12 mi) long, but the roads that climb the two sides of the valley are so winding that the whole circuit is more than 130 km (80 mi). The most famous viewpoint is the Belvédère de la Maline, although there are other stopping points around the gorge. The roads, especially that round the southern side of the gorge are full of switchbacks and tight turns, and a much more relaxing way to appreciate the views is to kayak along the river instead.

However, this area's main draw is its rocky cliffs and sheer drop, which are also very popular with rock climbers. There are more than 1,500 different climbs in the area, most of them far too difficult for beginners. There are also several designated hiking routes through the gorge, including the Sentier de l'Imbut, Sentier du Bastidon and that named after the valley's discoverer, the Sentier de Martel.

However you choose to spend your time in this beautiful landscape, you will not forget it easily.

*Kayaking along the river is a great way to appreciate the spectacular gorge.*

173

# Mercantour National Park

**WHAT IS IT?**
A beautiful, completely unspoiled region near the Côte d'Azure.

**HOW TO GET THERE:**
By bus from Menton.

**WHEN TO GO:**
The best time is from June to October.

**NEAREST TOWN:**
Monte-Carlo lies about 20 km (12.5 mi) to the south.

**DON'T MISS:**
Barcelonette, the Vallée des Merveilles, the Bronze-Age rock carvings near Mt Bégo.

This national park stretches for about 75 km (47 mi) in a narrow, mountainous ribbon between Barcelonette in the Alpes Maritimes to Sospel, about 20 km (12.5 mi) north of Monte-Carlo. Although it is almost completely uninhabited it is criss-crossed with trails and refuge huts for hikers.

The park contains several peaks, the highest being La Cime du Gélas at 3,143 m (10,312 ft), as well as the largest high-altitude lake in Europe, the Lac d'Allos. It is a beautiful, completely unspoiled area, with stunning waterfalls and gorges, but it is best known for its flora and fauna. Inland there are unusual Alpine plants such as the multi-flowering saxifrage as well as unique types of orchid and lily. Closer to the coast more typical *maquis* plant life can be found, the tough, aromatic species for which the Provencal hinterland is famous. The park is home to a host of Alpine mammals such as ibex, chamoix marmots, ermine, mouflon and reintroduced wolves. There are superb birds here too – golden eagles, peregrine falcons, hoopoes and ptarmigans.

Sospel, at the southern boundary, is a lovely,

peaceful town on the River Bevera. The place St-
Michel is a classic Provencal dream of peach-coloured
facades interspersed with two chapels and a
church, all overlooked by a ruined castle. This is a
splendid place in which to rest after hiking in the
high mountains.

*Autumn in Mercantour
National Park*

*Following pages: A
walker on the Col de la
Cayolle road admires the
view across Mercantour
National Park.*

175

# The Mountains of the Auvergne

The Auvergne is well known for the beauty of its wooded slopes and rocky peaks, particularly those of the Monts Dômes (also known as the Chaine des Puys) and the Mont Dore. What many do not realize, however, is that this stunning landscape in the Massif Central is a result of relatively recent volcanic

*A view across the spectacular Monts Dômes*

activity. The youngest, and highest, volcano in the Monts Dômes is the Puy-de-Dôme, which last erupted less than 8,000 years ago. This stunning mountain, with its double crater, is one of the most popular sights in France. A steep road spirals most of the way up the mountain, but the original Roman zigzag track to the top of this 1,464-m (4,803-ft) peak is popular with hikers. From the edge of the inner crater, the views north and south over the lava domes and cinder cones of the rest of the chain are stunning.

**WHAT IS IT?**
Chains of volcanoes in southern France.
**HOW TO GET THERE:**
By road from Lyon.
**WHEN TO GO:**
Any time of year.
**NEAREST TOWN:**
Clermont-Ferrand 10 km (6 mi).
**DON'T MISS:**
The cable-car ride and walk to the top of the Mont Dore.
**YOU SHOULD KNOW:**
Cycling on the Puy-de-Dôme is restricted to a few hours a week, when the road is closed to all other traffic.

*The Puy-de-Dôme*

To the south-west, the Monts Dorés are also volcanic. There are three main volcanoes – the Puy de Sancy, the Puy de l'Aiguiller and the Banne d'Ordanche, which dominate a landscape of woodland, lakes, rivers and waterfalls. This area was popular with the Romans because of its thermal springs and curative waters. There are still spas here today and the mineral-laced waters are exported the world over.

The Parc Naturel Régional des Volcans d'Auvergne is vast. It stretches from the Monts Dômes in the north to the Monts du Cantal in the south. This beautiful landscape is popular for hiking, canoeing and sailing in summer and skiing and snowboarding in winter.

# The Peak District

The Peak District stretches from the beautiful town of Ashbourne in the south to the craggy and remote High Peak District west of Sheffield. This, the first established of the National Parks, reaches deep into six English counties – Derbyshire, Cheshire, Staffordshire, South Yorkshire, West Yorkshire and Greater Manchester, but to most people The Peaks mean Derbyshire.

Rock dominates the landscape, in its pinnacles and spires and airy limestone crags that overhang the deep dales, whose greenness is counterpaned with grey-white dry stone walls and wandering threadlike rivers. The central core is the White Peak, limestone country, scarred everywhere by the green gorges of the dales. Surrounding this is an area of shale and thin sandstone through which rivers such as the Derwent and the Goyt have carved their wider, flatter valleys, and embracing all is the Dark Peak, sombre and forbidding, the gritstone rock rising to a moorland plateau – the lonely domain of red grouse and hardy sheep. Here are the Roaches – last bastion

**WHAT IS IT?**
A large area of hillscapes.
**HOW TO GET THERE:**
The M1 motorway runs to the east and north of the National Park and from junction 33 the A57 runs through the city of Sheffield and into the north of the Park which is also crossed by several major roads.
**WHEN TO GO:**
All year round.
**NEAREST TOWN:**
Ashbourne 10 km (6 mi) from Dovedale in the south Peak district.
**DON'T MISS:**
Mam Tor (Shivering Hill) the views from the cliff face at the top are stupendous.

*Sheep grazing in the Peak District.*

*Right: Heather in bloom on Curbar Edge*

of the Pennines – never rising to more than 518 m (1,700 ft) but with their fantastic ridge battlemented with weird, weathered shapes, this is a hugely impressive site.

Stone is everywhere in the architecture and the landscape, yet in contrast to this, the countryside is gentle, green and lush. Dove Dale is a wooded, utterly beautiful part of the valley of the Dove just to the north of Thorpe. Every part of the little river's course is extraordinarily pleasant and much of it can be followed by footpath. Thankfully, there are no riverside roads.

*Edale Valley*

# The Jurassic Coast

**WHAT IS IT?**
152 km (95 mi) of corroding south England coastline, showing ancient geological strata and fossils.

**HOW TO GET THERE:**
By train from London (Paddington) to Poole, Dorchester or Honiton or by road from London via the M3/A303 to Honiton.

**WHEN TO GO:**
All year round (busy in the summer months).

**NEAREST TOWN:**
Bridport 2.4 km (1.5 mi)

**DON'T MISS:**
Portland – a small island joined to Weymouth by a causeway and also the Fleet Lagoon at Chesil Beach.

**YOU SHOULD KNOW:**
Between Abbotsbury and Chesil Beach there is a tiny unused chapel on a hill called St Catherine's where spinsters come in November to wish for husbands.

This, the first British World Heritage Site, is 152 km (95 mi) of coast, recording 185 million years of ancient history through the Triassic, Jurassic and Cretaceous geological periods that comprise the Mesozoic Era. It stretches from the Orcombe Rocks in East Devon through to Studland Bay and Poole in West Dorset.

The cliff exposures along this coast provide an almost continuous sequence of rock formations spanning the Mesozoic Era. The area's important fossil sites and classic coastal geomorphologic features have greatly contributed to the study of earth sciences for over 300 years.

The Triassic period is seen from Exmouth to Lyme Regis, then the Jurassic from Lyme Regis to Swanage, and finally the Cretaceous period through to Studland Bay and into Poole harbour.

This area is also rich in wildlife with large populations of avocet, dark bellied Brent goose, Slavonian grebe and the little tern at Chesil Beach. The Lulworth Skipper butterfly can be spotted amongst the early spider orchid, gentian, wild cabbage and the Nottingham catchfly. There is a long history of mining for shale, and local stone from Portland, Beer and Purbeck have been used

throughout the UK for building work.

The Jurassic Coast, and in particular Lyme Regis and Charmouth with their clay based old tropical seas with soft, muddy and often stagnant lower levels, was perfect for preserving shells, bones and even soft tissue of long dead prehistoric creatures. Imagine the excitement of discovering green ammonites and 197 million-year-old Belamnite Marl alongside other vertebrate and invertebrate marine and terrestrial fossils, and even ancient fossilized footprints.

*A fossil ammonite on the Jurassic Coast in the Lyme Regis area of Dorset*

*Following pages: The cliffs at Burton Bradstock lit by the setting sun*

185

# Lundy

Some 19 km (12 mi) out in the Bristol Channel, where the Atlantic Ocean meets the Severn River, lies the island of Lundy. Protected by its high, granite cliffs and remote location, the island has a colourful past. Today it belongs to the National Trust, is leased to the Landmark Trust, and its solitary and beautiful nature brings visitors back here over and over again.

Lundy has been inhabited since pre-historic times, and has suffered endless disputes over its ownership. In 1242, Henry III built a castle here to consolidate his control – instead Lundy became anarchic and chaos reigned until William Hudson Heaven bought the island in 1834. He erected many of the buildings, including St Helena's Church but sold the island to Martin Harman, a naturalist, in 1925. Harman transformed Lundy, and the National Trust acquired the island from his children in 1969.

The island consists of open moorland in the north, some farmland and a village to the south. Some 20,000 visitors come here each year, for the day or to stay in one of the 23 beautifully restored buildings that include a lighthouse and the castle. Those spending longer here can walk the glorious 11 km (7 mi) coastal path, admiring the surrounding waters that form Britain's first Marine Nature Reserve. Marine life is exceedingly rich – in particular there are rare species of seaweed, corals and fans. Grey seals are much in evidence, and basking sharks can also be spotted.

Much of Lundy is an area of Special Scientific Interest, and the flora and fauna are rich and varied. It has its own endemic species of cabbage, and its own distinct breed of Lundy pony. It is also, naturally, bliss for birders. Although puffins are now few, the cliffs are home to thousands of seabirds, and in spring and autumn rare visitors occasionally appear, having been blown off course during migration.

**WHAT IS IT?**
An island in the Bristol Channel much of which is an area of Special Scientific Interest.

**HOW TO GET THERE:**
By ferry from Bideford or Ilfracombe, or (November to March) helicopter from Hartland Point.

**WHEN TO GO:**
Any time, but April to November is probably best.

**DON'T MISS:**
The disused granite quarries.
The Devil's Slide – great for rock climbing.
The three lighthouses – one of which you can stay in, the other two are functioning.
Diving over the wrecks and enjoying other water sports such as surfing.

**YOU SHOULD KNOW:**
In 1929 Martin Harman issued his own Lundy postage stamps, their value expressed in 'puffins'. These stamps are still printed today, but must be stuck on an envelope's bottom left hand corner, their cost includes Royal Mail's charges. Known as 'local carriage labels' in the world of philately, some of Lundy's stamps are now highly prized.

*An aerial view of Lundy*

189

# Snowdon and Snowdonia

**WHAT IS IT?**
Wales's highest mountain,
set in a stunning
landscape.
**HOW TO GET THERE:**
By road from Caernarfon or
rail from Llanberis.
**WHEN TO GO:**
April to October
**NEAREST TOWN:**
Llanberis 5 km (3 mi)
**DON'T MISS:**
The amazing views from
the summit.
**YOU SHOULD KNOW:**
It takes about five hours to
get to the top of the
mountain on foot.

*A cobblestone trail
above Capel Curig
in Snowdonia*

At 1,085 m (3,560 ft), Snowdon is the highest mountain
in Wales, and the fourth highest in the British Isles. The
Snowdonia National Park was formed in 1951 to
protect an area 56 by 80 km (35 by 50 mi), which
covers most of north-west Wales.

Snowdon itself is one of the most popular
mountains in Britain for climbers, but the less energetic
can get to the summit by catching the Snowdon
Mountain Railway from Llanberis in the west. There are
half a dozen routes up the mountain, so pick one that
suits your ability. There are also walking, hiking, pony
and mountain-biking and cycling trails lower down the
mountain and throughout the park.

The views from the top of the mountain are
unbelievable, but there is also stunning scenery lower
down, from woodland to secluded valleys with gushing

waterfalls. The weather can often be worse up in the
high peaks, so if the weather forecast is not good, other
activities such as white-water rafting, sailing and pony
trekking are on offer. There are 37 km (23 mi) of sandy
beaches to enjoy on the Lleyn peninsula.

The park is home to a wide variety of wildlife,
including otters in the lower rivers, a good range of
butterflies in the wildflower meadows, important
populations of the minute lesser horseshoe bat,
buzzards, peregrine falcons and many smaller species of
birds, and the feral goats that have roamed the area for
at least 10,000 years.

*The Snowdon Mountain
Railway is a great way
to reach the summit.*

*Following pages: A view
to Llynnau Mymbyr
and the Snowdon
Horsehoe*

**191**

*Llanberis Pass cuts through the Snowdonia range.*

# The Small Isles

Collectively known as the Small Isles, Eigg, Rhum, Muck, Canna and Sanday are tranquil gems, situated to the south of Skye. The dominant feature of Eigg, (pronounced egg) the Sgurr of Eigg, is a basalt peak formed from columnar lava, which rises to 393 m (1,297 ft) from the plateau which makes up most of the rest of the island. In 1997 the islanders managed to buy Eigg from its owner, having launched an appeal and formed a partnership with the Highland Council and the Scottish Wildlife Trust.

Rhum is the largest and most mountainous of the islands, and is a Scottish Natural Heritage nature reserve. Permission has to be sought before visiting, but once there, you can trek the nature trails and enjoy glorious scenery. The flora and fauna here are special – the spotted orchid is an endemic sub-species. Rhum has its own herd of ponies, as well as Highland cattle, feral goats and red deer, and it is twitcher heaven, especially since the SNH have successfully reintroduced the magnificent white-tailed sea eagle, its wingspan exceeding even that of the golden eagle, which can also, occasionally be seen.

Muck is a miniscule – just 3 km (2 mi) by 1.6 km (1 mi) – privately owned, gorgeous island. In spring the machair is a blanket of wild flowers, and the beaches glitter with white shell sand. At Gallanach Bay, such bliss, you can watch otters and porpoises play.

Canna and Sanday are joined by a footbridge, and the area between them forms the best harbour in the Small Isles. Owned by the National Trust for Scotland, Canna is run both as a bird sanctuary and a farm, and visitors to the island come to walk. Originally wooded with rowan and hazel, spruce, pine, oak, larch and other trees have been introduced. Puffins and Manx shearwater breed on the western cliffs, and altogether 157 bird species have been recorded here.

**WHAT IS IT?**
Five tranquil islands south of Skye.
**HOW TO GET THERE:**
By ferry from Mallaig
**WHEN TO GO:**
Any time, but May to September is possibly best.
**DON'T MISS:**
Massacre Cave and Cathedral Cave (especially if a Mass is being said) on Eigg.
Kinloch Castle and the Bullugh Mausoleum on Rhum.
The views over the Small Isles from the top of Ben Airean on Muck.
The Celtic Cross and ruins of St Columba's Chapel on Canna.
**YOU SHOULD KNOW:**
Ferries to the Small Isles do not operate on Sundays.

*Following pages: A view to the Small Isles of Rum, Eigg and Muck from Sanna Bay in the Highlands*

# The Cairngorms

**WHAT IS IT?**
A mountain range in the Highlands of Scotland.
**HOW TO GET THERE:**
By train, air or road to Aberdeen then take the A93 to Braemar, which is in the Cairngorm National Park.

The Cairngorm Mountains lie in the Cairngorm National Park, which is often described as having some of the most spectacular landscapes in Britain, from the wild tundra of the high mountaintops to the seclusion of ancient pinewoods and heather. Here, too, is moorland, vivid with summer colour, and grand glens and rivers all scarred by glacial action.

The name Cairngorm derives from the Gaelic for

'The Blue Hills' while the range of mountains were called Monadh Ruadh or 'The Red Hills' due to the reddish hue of their granite composition. The eighteen mountains are part of the Munros and are amongst the highest in the country. They were formed in the last ice age with static ice caps shaping the rounded mountaintops and they are drained by the Dee and Spey rivers and the latter's tributaries, the Feshie and the Avon.

There is little population due to the harsh climate,

**WHEN TO GO:**
All year round.
**NEAREST TOWN:**
Aberdeen 96 km (60 mi)
**DON'T MISS:**
The single malt whiskies.
**YOU SHOULD KNOW:**
The unpredictable weather can be dangerous especially in the winter.

*Loch an Eilein*

*Lochindorb on
Dava Moor*

with snow on the hills – sometimes until August, but
the wildlife is wonderful. Here are red and roe deer,
the only wild reindeer in Britain, mountain hare, pine
marten, red squirrel, wild cat and otter all surveyed
by the magnificent golden eagle, ospreys, ptarmigan,
the rare cap dotterel, with snowy owl, purple
sandpiper and Lapland bunting seen on occasion.

The valley, the Lairg Ghru Pass, is an old drovers'
route to the Lowlands and the mighty salmon-laden
River Spey runs down to the sea overlooked by
Cairngorm itself, and other rivers supply the pure
water for malt whiskies such as Glenlivet. A funicular
railway transports passengers to the Ptarmigan
centre, 150 m (490 ft) from the summit of Cairngorm,
giving easy access for hill walkers, winter sports
enthusiasts, climbers, birdwatchers and deer stalkers.
Fly-fishing and hang gliding are amongst other
pursuits but it must be remembered that the
Highlands can be a dangerous and hazardous place
with unpredictable weather.

*Right: Loch Morlich and
the Cairngorms
in winter*

# The Dingle Peninsula

**WHAT IS IT?**
The most westerly point of Ireland.
**HOW TO GET THERE:**
By road from Tralee or Castlemaine.
**WHEN TO GO:**
Summer but pack a raincoat!
**NEAREST TOWN:**
Dingle
**DON'T MISS:**
Fungie the dolphin.
**YOU SHOULD KNOW:**
The drive from Dingle over the Connor Pass is not for the faint-hearted.

The northernmost of the five peninsulas that project out into the Atlantic like fingers at the south-west tip of Ireland, the Dingle Peninsula (Corca Dhuibhne) is the westernmost point of mainland Ireland. It lies on a sandstone ridge that also forms the Slieve Mish mountains in the east of the peninsula and Mount Brandon, Ireland's second highest mountain at 953 m (3,127 ft).

Often beset by the weather that the North Atlantic throws at it, this wild landscape is known for its spectacular scenery with stunning views of the Great Blasket Island, Dingle Bay and across Castlemaine Harbour to MacGillicuddy Reeks. Described by many

as one of the most beautiful landscapes on Earth, it has rocky outcrops and rugged cliffs, soft rounded hills with forests, beautiful alpine-arctic flora higher up and wide sandy beaches. There is a magnificent view around almost every corner. Off the beaten track, there are many side roads and paths that allow visitors to explore this breathtaking countryside at their leisure.

In spring and early summer, seabirds such as gannets nest on the cliffs, while Fungie the dolphin has lived in the harbour since 1984.

Popular activities include walking, boat trips out to the Great Blasket Island, swimming, surfing, walking or horse-riding through the edge of the surf. There are also hundreds of archaeological sites to visit.

*Following pages: A view out to sea from the rugged Dingle Peninsula*

*The stunning coastline of the Dingle Peninsula*

# The Balkan Mountains

**WHAT IS IT?**
A range of mountains
extending from Serbia
through northern Bulgaria
to the Black Sea.
**HOW TO GET THERE:**
By road or train.
**WHEN TO GO:**
July, August and
September.
**NEAREST TOWN:**
There are many towns and
villages in these
mountains.
**DON'T MISS:**
The historic monasteries
and their treasures.
**YOU SHOULD KNOW:**
Even during the summer
the weather is
unpredictable.

The Balkan Mountains, or
Stara Planina, extend some
560 km (350 mi) from
eastern Serbia, through
northern Bulgaria, to Cape
Emin, which lies to the
north of Burgas, on the
Black Sea. The highest
peaks are in the central
section, and include Mount
Botev, at 2,376 m (7,795
ft), as well as 20 others
that pass the 2,000 m
(6,600 ft) level. Rivers
from the Balkan Mountains
mainly flow north to the
Danube, or south to the
Aegean Sea, and 20 passes
and several railway lines
cross the range.

The region is notable
for its flora and fauna, and
includes nine nature reserves, four of which are
UNESCO Biosphere reserves. Ancient forests of
hornbeam, beech, spruce, fir and durmast cloak the
slopes of the Central Balkan National Park, giving
shelter to ten species and two sub-species of flora
that are endemic. Edelweiss grows here, 256 species
of mushroom can be found, and 166 species of
medicinal plant. The mountains are full of birds – 224
different species – making the region a magnet for
twitchers. The scenery is varied: there are very lovely,
high, mountain meadows filled with wild flowers,
waterfalls that tumble and splash down almost

*Central Balkan National Park*

vertical rock faces, deep, mysterious canyons and exciting caves.

These mountains have been inhabited for centuries and there are several towns enabling the visitor to discover the region's cultural and historical heritage. It is also known for its monasteries, some of which were founded as long ago as the 12th century. Within their walls lie many treasures – icons, frescoes and fabulously carved wooden iconostases. During the 19th century many monks were actively engaged in the national liberation struggle, and many of the monasteries were destroyed and later restored.

*Lubenice Beach*

# Cres

One of the largest of the 1,200 islands along the Croatian coast, Cres is situated in the Gulf of Kvarner to the east of Istria. It is long, narrow and mountainous, stretching 68 km (43 mi) from north to south and 12 km (8 mi) across at its widest point. The inaccessible sheer rock face of the spectacular east coast cliffs are a habitat for the griffon vulture, the largest bird in

Europe. The northern hills are cloaked in woodland of oak, hornbeam, elm and chestnut, in stunning contrast to the grazing pastures, olive groves and pine thickets further south. In the middle of the island there is the mysterious natural phenomenon of Lake Vrana. It is the main source of fresh water for both Cres and the neighbouring islands, but geologists cannot explain where its 220 million cu m (7,766 million cu ft) of water comes from.

There is evidence of Neolithic habitation: traces of cave dwellings and Bronze and Iron Age hill-forts and tumuli. The Romans conquered the island during the reign of the Emperor Augustus and later it became part of the Byzantine Empire. For several hundred years it was ruled by Venice before falling under the sway of the Austro-Hungarian Empire, eventually becoming integrated into Croatia in 1945. The island's cultural heritage can be seen in the picturesque villages and the charming main town of Cres where there are plenty of remnants of the island's Venetian era.

Surrounded by a tranquil, clear blue sea, with isolated bays and rocky coves, this wild, sparsely populated island is scenically dotted with old ruins, cemeteries and chapels; crumbling dry-stone walls follow the contours of hills on which a huge diversity of native plants can be found. Cres is an ecotourist delight.

**WHAT IS IT?**
The second largest island in the Adriatic.
**HOW TO GET THERE:**
The nearest international airports are Trieste, Pula and Zagreb. Cres can only be reached by boat, either directly on the 12 times daily ferry from Brestova, on the Istrian peninsula, or via the islands of Losinj or Krk.
**WHEN TO GO:**
April to October.
**DON'T MISS:**
The walk from Stivan to Ustrine – takes 2½ hours, or turn it into a full day.
Lubenice – an ancient village with a really beautiful view.
Beli – one of the oldest settlements on the island with an Eco-Centre.
The view from Gorice – the highest point of the island at 650 m (2,130 ft).
**YOU SHOULD KNOW:**
The shores of Cres are pebble, which is probably the reason why the island has managed to avoid the full glare of the holiday industry and to retain its pristine natural environment. Don't let the lack of sand put you off. The beaches are clean, uncrowded and excellent for swimming and scuba diving.

# Macocha Gorge

**WHAT IS IT?**
Natural limestone gorge.
**HOW TO GET THERE:**
Flights, trains, buses to
Bratislava or Brno then
take the E461 to Lipuvka,
the 374 to Blansko and on
to Vilemovice, which is in
the Moravian Karst.
**WHEN TO GO:**
May to September
**NEAREST TOWN:**
Brno 40 km (25 mi)
**DON'T MISS:**
Balcarka Cave

This is a wonderful area of Moravian Karst with a multitude of caves, underground streams and dead-end valleys. The karst's best-known features are the Punkva Cave and the Macocha Gorge, located north of the city of Brno, in the Drahanska Highlands.

The Macocha Gorge, from the Czech 'Propast Macocha' – literally 'the 'stepmother gorge', is also known as the Macocha Abyss. Part of its beauty is that it is formed by a roof collapse of an underground cave forming a 'light hole' filtering light down into the abyss below.

The history of the name 'stepmother' comes from a 17th century legend of a widower living with his son. On remarrying, his new wife bore him a child, but wishing to be rid of her stepson, she threw him over the abyss. Fortunately he was caught in the branches below and saved by local woodcutters. Hearing the woodcutters' story, the village people of Vilemovice threw the stepmother over the abyss and killed her.

The gorge is a 'doline' or sinkhole, 139 m (455 ft) deep, the deepest of this type in Central Europe. The limestone from which it is formed is 350 – 380 million years old and there are as many as 1,000 caves that have been discovered in this region. These are referred to as the Amateur caves.

This area forms part of the Punkva Natural Reserve and is not open to traffic, but tourists and hikers can see the interiors and the beautiful stalagmites and stalactites of the Punkva caves on the Punkva River, which leads to the bottom of the Macocha Gorge. Take a trip on an electric boat on the green waters of the river, through the Macocha caves and the nearby Katerina Cave, with a stop over in the Masaryk chamber.

*Punkevní jeskyne cave*

**WHAT IS IT?**
The biggest untouched
boreal forest in Europe.
**HOW TO GET THERE:**
By air, rail or bus to
Pechora; by road to
Troitsko-Pechorsk.
**WHEN TO GO:**
May to September.
**NEAREST TOWN:**
Pechora (N) or Troitsko-
Pechorsk (S)
**DON'T MISS:**
The moss swamps of the
piedmont.
**YOU SHOULD KNOW:**
Moose milk is medicinal.

# Virgin Komi Forests

The Virgin Komi Forests cover 3.28 million hectares
(8.1 million acres) of tundra and mountain tundra in
the northern Urals, the most extensive area of virgin
boreal forest remaining in Europe. Almost completely
undisturbed by economic activities, the region is a
real treasure trove of taiga biodiversity. It accounts
for over 40 species of mammals like the brown bear,
sable, moose, ermine, arctic fox and wolverine
(skunk bear); 204 species of birds including the
endangered white sea eagle and fish hawk; and
valuable fish like the glacial relic species, the lake
char and arctic grayling.

The Virgin Komi Biosphere unites two major sites:
the Pechoro-Ilychsky
Nature Preserve and the
enormous Yugyd-Va
National Park. Their
combined territory
stretches for 300 km (188
mi) along the western
slope of the Polar and
Northern Urals, marking
the transition of mid- and
northern taiga to forest
and mountain tundra, and
the north-western limit of
the Siberian cedar's
habitat. Their position is
important to the entire
regional ecosystem: the
humid western slopes
contribute to the great
Pechora River basin
where European plant
species abruptly replace
the Siberian flora of the

*Virgin boreal forest in
the Polar Urals*

eastern Urals. Among the Pechora piedmont of spruce, pine and fir forests are both pine and moss swamps, and the Gusinoe Bolota (Goose Swamp) is a 3 sq km (1.2 sq mi) peat bog over 5 m (16 ft) deep, near which a small research establishment is still conducting experiments in domesticating moose.

Current attempts to have the Biosphere's borders moved to legalize the prospecting and mining of gold have failed; only time will tell if the regional Supreme Court can withstand the machinations of the self-same regional government, which seeks the change.

*A view of forest and mountain tundra*

# Kuril Islands

**WHAT IS IT?**
A chain of volcanic islands.
**HOW TO GET THERE:**
You need a lot of determination to get to the Kuril Islands. By boat to Kunashir (the southernmost island) from Kushiro, north Japan. Irregular ferry services to the other inhabited islands and a once monthly boat from Korsakov, the southern port of Sakhalin Island, Eastern Russia. To explore the Kurils thoroughly you must charter a boat or join an eco-expedition.
**WHEN TO GO:**
June to October
**NEAREST TOWN:**
Kurilsk, on the island of Iturup, is the largest village in the Kurils.
**DON'T MISS:**
Alaid Volcano – the highest point of the Kurils at 2,339 m (7,672 ft) on Atlasov Island, a near perfect symmetrical cone rising straight out of the sea, considered to be even more beautiful than Mount Fuji.
Tao-Rusyr Caldera, Onekotan – 7.5 km (nearly 5 mi) diameter with lake and dome.
Golovnin Volcano, Kunashir – crater of 4 km (2.5 mi) diameter with boiling lake.
**YOU SHOULD KNOW:**
The Kurils were discovered in 1634 and first charted in 1739. They were seized by Japan in the 19th century and only returned to Russia at the end of World War II.

This chain of 56 volcanic islands stretches for almost 1,300 km (700 mi) like stepping-stones all the way from the Kamatchka Peninsula to Hokkaido, Japan. They form the boundary between the Sea of Okhotsk and the Pacific Ocean and are the summits of undersea stratovolcanoes, part of the Pacific Ring of Fire. Offshore is the Kuril Trench, one of the deepest ocean regions of the world, 10.5 km (6.4 mi) deep.

The Kurils are astoundingly beautiful with dense vegetation except at the highest elevations and an amazing variety of spectacular scenery ranging from dramatic volcanic ridges and craters to alpine tundra, meadows and wetland. There are broadleaf woods, coniferous forests, crater lakes enclosed by trees, lush narrow valleys and fast running streams with coasts of steep cliffs, volcanic sand beaches and rocky shores. Many millions of seabirds congregate on every available hummock and cliff ledge during the breeding season, and the seas are rich in marine life including shoals of orcas, Baird's whales, fin and sperm whales, sea otters, sealions and fur seals.

Forty of the islands are volcanically active, with fumaroles, hot springs and frequent eruptions. The remainder are sparsely

inhabited, mainly by fishermen scraping a subsistence living in a severe climate of blistering winter winds and summer fogs with the ever-present possibility of earthquakes, tsunamis and sulphurous eruptions. A combination of distance from the mainland, the depth of the ocean and strong currents have been major barriers to plant and animal dispersal so that each island has its own self-contained ecosystem and natural history. The Kurils are in one of the least scientifically explored regions of the world – an eco-adventurer's paradise, full of unique biological and geological wonders.

*Following pages:
Tao-Rusyr Caldera,
Onekotan*

*The Kuril Islands are
an eco-adventurer's
paradise.*

**WHAT IS IT?**
A beautiful, but isolated, chain of islands – the most northerly point of Europe.
**HOW TO GET THERE:**
On a cruise boat from Spitzbergen (Svaalbard)
**WHEN TO GO:**
July to August
**DON'T MISS:**
Cape Flora, Nordbrook Island – sea bird colony. Rubini Rock, Hooker Island. Stolichky and Appolonov Islands – walrus rookeries. Alger and Wilczek Islands – polar bears.
**YOU SHOULD KNOW:**
A trip to Franz Josef Land is an extreme adventure. It is a Russian military zone and you can only go there on an escorted expedition. Landing on the islands is entirely dependent on weather conditions.

# Franz Josef Land

A strangely compelling world of icebergs, glaciers and the Midnight Sun, Franz Josef Land is one of the few remaining truly wild places on the planet. It is an archipelago of 191 volcanic islands, indented with dramatic bays and fjords, covering an area of 16,130 sq km (6,290 sq mi) in the Barents Sea, almost entirely within the Arctic Circle. Here is the most northerly point of Europe, only 911 km (569 mi) from the North Pole, at Cape Fligely on Rudolph Island.

A pair of Austrian explorers, Julius Payer and Karl Weyprecht landed here in 1873 and named the archipelago Franz Joseph Land in honour of their Emperor. But Austria never claimed the territory and in 1926 the Soviet Union won a race against Norway to gain sovereignty; it now belongs to Russia. Apart from a meteorological station on Zemlya Aleksandri (Alexandra Land), the westernmost island, the islands

*An iceberg in the truly wild Franz Josef Land*

are uninhabited. Over a fifty-year period, the highest temperature recorded is 13 °C (55.4 °F) and the lowest is -54 °C (-65.2 °F).

In the summer months the icy sea takes on a crazy mosaic appearance. Almost 85 per cent of the land surface is permanently glaciated with an ice layer averaging 180 m (590 ft) thick. The only colour to be seen in this blinding ice-white wilderness is in the extraordinary reds and greens of the lichens and mosses that cling to the stark rocky outcrops. The dramatic scenery is at its most majestic on Champ Island in the centre of the archipelago. Here are the highest cliffs and mountains of the archipelago and extraordinary boulders – perfectly spherical and up to 3 m (10 ft) in diameter. The unforgiving climate supports arctic foxes, walruses, polar bears and beluga whales, and 37 bird species including kittiwakes and fulmars. A trip to Franz Josef Land is a unique and unforgettable experience.

*Left: A polar bear roams the sea ice.*

# Mountains of Majorca

**WHAT IS IT?**
Rugged mountains in the north west of Majorca.
**HOW TO GET THERE:**
By train.
**WHEN TO GO**
April to May or September
**NEAREST TOWN:**
Sóller
**YOU SHOULD KNOW:**
The Serra de Tramuntana is brilliant walking country with well-marked trails to suit all levels of ability.

*A wildflower meadow beneath Tramuntana mountains*

The reality of Majorca belies its reputation as a high-rise hell of commercialized tourism. Apart from the narrow coastal strip along the Bay of Palma and the grim east coast resorts, the island is startlingly beautiful, particularly in the Serra de Tramuntana, the rugged mountains of the north-west. Here are soaring peaks interspersed with valleys of olive and citrus groves, sheer cliffs plunging into the sea, and charming mountain villages tucked away in the hills.

By far the most enjoyable way of travelling to the mountains is to catch the quaint little antique train from Palma to Sóller, originally built for the orange merchants of Sóller who needed a more efficient means of getting to the island capital than the long circuitous haul across the mountains by horse and cart. The train has been running since 1912 and its

mahogany panelled, brass-fitted wooden carriages take you a step back in time as you make the 28 km (17.5 mi) journey along a narrow gauge track through staggeringly beautiful countryside. The train winds its way northwards across the plain of Palma and climbs into the mountains across enchanting valleys thick with citrus groves. It stops at villages along the way and there are some astounding views as well as scarily long sections of tunnel that only end after you've begun to think they're never going to.

Sóller is a lovely mountain town, built on a slope around a main square with several cafés and bars. The town has miraculously retained a genuine, un-touristy atmosphere about it and you stroll through sleepy narrow streets of 18th and 19th century stone houses with huge wooden doors and wrought iron *rejas* (screens). It is a brilliant base for hiking expeditions or you can take an old-fashioned tram down to the coast.

*Following pages:*
*Almond trees in blossom*
*beneath the mountains*

# Ordesa Y Monte Perdido National Park

**WHAT IS IT?**
One of Spain's earliest national parks.
**HOW TO GET THERE:**
By road from Zaragoza.
**WHEN TO GO:**
Summer
**NEAREST TOWN:**
Sabiñánigo 40 km (25 mi)
**YOU SHOULD KNOW:**
Don't stray over the border into France without your passport.

At the very top of the Pyrenees, lies the massif of the Three Sisters (Tres Sorores), whose highest crests form the border with France. From these heights, glacial valleys radiate out, between crests and gradually the bare heights give way to rough meadows with typical wildflowers including edelweiss, then black pine woodlands, then beech, oak, ash, birch and fir in the valley bottoms far below. The park adjoins the Parc National des Pyrénées across the border, and together they form a UNESCO World Heritage Site. The limestone landscape is full of gorges and caves hewn out of the rock by water, while in the heights glacial cirques are reminders of the forces that created this landscape. The glacier on the north side of Monte Perdido is retreating rapidly, and those on the south have long since disappeared.

Although the Pyrenean ibex is thought to have become extinct in the area recently, several other species are still to be found, including marmots, otters, wild boar and a species of water-mole called the Pyrenean desman. There is plenty for the birdwatcher: the walls of gorges are good places to look for the lovely pink of the wallcreeper, while dipper should be common on rocks in mountain streams. Larger birds seen in the area at various times include short-toed, golden and booted eagles and honey buzzard, as well as lammergeier and griffon vulture that soar up over the high peaks.

*Glacial valleys and rough meadows make up the landscape of the Ordesa Y Monte Perdido National Park.*

*Anisclo Canyon*

# Teide

Away from the towns of Tenerife, the largest of the Canary Islands, it is difficult to escape the sight of the island's central volcano. As you travel round the base of it through lush green plantations, it is always there, in the corner of your eye. At 3,718 m (11,823 ft), it is the tallest mountain in Spain and the tallest volcano in Europe. It is a stratovolcano, sitting on a hotspot in the eastern Atlantic and the last eruption, from one of the side vents, occurred as recently as 1909. Fumaroles at the top emit hot gases such as sulphur dioxide so visitors are not allowed in the crater.

Some 150,000 years ago, a far larger eruption caused the collapse of the previous cone, leaving a caldera 10 by 15 km (6 by 9 mi) across and up to 600 m (1,970 ft) deep. The current peak derives from a later eruption. The floor of the caldera has strange rock formations that stick up like thumbs and result from later erosion.

The views from the cable car station across the lunar landscape of the caldera are breathtaking: two short paths allow visitors to access viewpoints but you must have a permit to climb the last 200 m (660 ft) to the peak.

**WHAT IS IT?**
The tallest volcano in Europe.
**HOW TO GET THERE:**
By road from Santa Cruz de Tenerife or via the cable car to La Rambleta.
**WHEN TO GO:**
Spring to autumn
**NEAREST TOWN:**
Granadilla de Abona 20 km (12 mi)
**DON'T MISS:**
The views.
**YOU SHOULD KNOW:**
You need a permit to climb to the peak itself and entry to the crater is strictly forbidden.

*Pico de Teide*

*Following pages: An aerial view of the Pico Viejo, Teide National Park*

*An aerial view of Stromboli*

# Stromboli

**WHAT IS IT?**
An active volcanic island.
**HOW TO GET THERE:**
Fly to Catania in Sicily then bus/train to Milazzo or Messina and ferry/hydrofoil to Lipari; or, from mainland Italy, ferry/hydrofoil from Reggio di Calabria or Naples to Lipari. Boat from Lipari to Stromboli.
**WHEN TO GO:**
April to mid-June to see the island at its most beautiful.

Stromboli is the summit of a volcanic mountain sticking 926 m (2,950 ft) out of the Tyrrhenian Sea. The rest of it is submerged to a depth of 1,500 m (4,920 ft). It is the most remote of the Aeolian Islands, a volcanic archipelago off the northern coast of Sicily, about 50 km (30 mi) from the Italian mainland.

'The Lighthouse of the Mediterranean' is one of the most active volcanoes on the planet – it has been in a state of more or less constant eruption for the past 2,000 years. The volcano stands alone in the middle of the sea, emitting a constant plume of steam from its cone. At night, there is the awesome spectacle of its flame shooting into the sky, like a giant firework.

Constant minor explosions throw incandescent blobs of lava over the crater rim several times an hour, and the term 'Strombolian eruption' is used to describe this sort of volcanic activity anywhere.

Amazingly, this tiny island, only 12.6 sq km (5 sq mi), is inhabited by about 500 people, who live philosophically in the shadow of the volcano in two villages and several tiny hamlets perched on its slopes. The views from the upper slopes are stunning – rugged cliffs tower above the black sand beaches and you gaze across a clear blue sea dotted with islands.

Throughout Stromboli's long history, large eruptions and lava flows have been rare. There was one in 2002 for the first time in 17 years, which created the Sciara di Fuoco (Slope of Fire), a horseshoe-shaped crater, and caused two landslides and several tsunami waves up to 10 m (33 ft) high. In February 2007, two new craters opened, with lava flowing into the sea from one of them. Since then, Stromboli has been under extra surveillance.

**NEAREST TOWN:**
Lipari town, Island of Lipari
34 km (21 mi)
**DON'T MISS:**
A guided trip to the crater, if possible at sunset.
**YOU SHOULD KNOW:**
Stromboli was the setting for Jules Verne's novel *A Journey to the Centre of the Earth*.
The Aeolian Islands are named after Aeolus, god of the winds.

*Stromboli is one of the most active volcanoes on the planet.*

*The Loggerhead is the largest of all sea turtles swimming the oceans today.*

# Loggerhead Turtles, Zakynthos

Of the eight species of sea turtle swimming the oceans today, the Loggerhead (*Caretta caretta*) is the largest. Recognizable by its big head, reddish-brown shell and yellow underside, an average Loggerhead weighs more than 100 kg (220 lbs) and is 120 cm (4 ft) in length. Greece is the only country within Europe where these turtles nest, and the sandy beaches of Laganas Bay, on the island of Zakynthos, host the largest nesting colony of this endangered species.

Little is known about the life of sea turtles, particularly the males. We do know that they live for about 60 years, reaching reproductive age at about 30, and that Loggerheads make the longest migration journeys of all sea turtle species. Their strong jaws can easily crush their food – largely shellfish or jellyfish. Nesting females can be tagged to provide information about migration routes, but males never leave the sea.

At night, between June and August, the female Loggerheads drag themselves up the beach to lay some 200 eggs in nests of 40 – 60 cm (1ft 4 ins – 2 ft) deep, which they cover with warm sand. This process is repeated three or four times each season. About eight weeks later, the eggs hatch, and the hatchlings scrabble up through the sand and dash to the sea. After this their lives are unknown until, some 30 years later, the females return to the same beach to reproduce.

In 1999 a National Marine Park was established in southern Zakynthos to protect about 6 km (4 mi) of separate, sandy beaches where about 900 turtles come to nest each year. Sadly, by 2004, the management body had ceased to function, and so many violations of the protection laws were occurring that the European Commission began legal action against the Greek authorities, who appeared to feel that tourism was more important than protecting these desperately important breeding sites.

**WHAT IS IT?**
The only European nesting grounds of the Loggerhead turtle.

**HOW TO GET THERE:**
By plane or boat to the island, then by car.

**WHEN TO GO:**
Between June and October for the Loggerhead's reproductive season.

**NEAREST TOWN:**
Keri

**DON'T MISS:**
The Blue Caves on the Skinari Cape; the Venetian Castle in Bohali; the Monastery of St George at Gremna; the Strofadia islands 35 km (22 mi) south of Zakynthos.

**YOU SHOULD KNOW:**
Many restrictions apply to the protected areas, which include boating and water sports within the sea itself.

*Turtles come to nest on the sandy beaches of Zakynthos.*

# Pamukkale

Visible from kilometres away, the dazzling 100-m (330-ft) white cliff of Pamukkale is one of the geological wonders of the world. Water from hot springs on the volcanic plateau above bubbles out of the ground at 35 °C (95 °F) and streams down the side of the cliff, depositing calcium carbonate in the form of blinding white travertine as it cools and creates strangely shaped terraces and pools as it goes.

Pamukkale means 'Cotton Fortress' and according to legend the white cliffs were created when the giant Titans left their crop of cotton out to dry. Over thousands of years, the terraces have grown out from the cliff like a magical giant staircase or solid waterfall. Everywhere you go, you are accompanied by the sound of splashing water.

Because of earlier damage to the soft, porous rock, only a few terraces are open to the public, but paths lead right round the site. At the top of the cliff, it is possible to bathe in the town's thermal baths, which include the original sacred spring. As you swim about, you can see the water bubbling out of the ground beneath you.

The site, and the supposedly health-giving effects of the water, have been known about for thousands of years and the ruins of ancient Hierapolis, which grew up around the spring, dot the top of the cliff. Close to the baths is the Plutonium, a grotto sacred to the god of the underworld. From the grille that prevents entry, you can hear rushing water and the hiss of the poisonous gas that escapes from the ground here.

*Right: The striking terraces of Pamukkale*

*Following pages: Sunset above the sinter terraces in Pamukkale*

# Göreme National Park

In the heart of Cappadocia, Göreme National Park has one of the strangest landscapes on earth. Over millions of years, volcanoes in the area covered the land with thick layers of soft tuff stone, which were then covered with layers of lava that hardened and sealed the top. Eventually, water broke through and the soft rock below became subject to weathering, and wind, snow and rain have carved it into conical pillars, towers and needles of varying colours and heights of up to 40–50 m (130–165 ft). The volcanic plain once covered some 10,000 sq km (3,850 sq mi) of landscape and the park now protects the central 95 sq km (37 sq mi). The soft rock is also easily carved by humans and over the centuries many of the pillars, the so-called fairy chimneys, have been turned into homes or churches, and the latter are famous for their Byzantine murals.

Away from the villages, the landscape is best explored on foot or by bicycle. A popular walk is the 12-km (7.5-mi) circuitous path to Üçhisar through the Uzundere Valley. The valleys are dominated by the volcanoes that produced the landscape, such as Erciyas Dag and Hasan Dag.

Up in the hills of this spectacular valley, wolves and beech martens can sometimes be spotted, and badgers, foxes and hares also inhabit the park.

Although it is expensive, a popular way to get a grasp on the whole landscape – and to get amazing photographs – is to take one of the many balloon trips on offer. Drifting over this weird landscape on a clear, still morning is a magical experience.

*Following pages: A view over rock chimneys in the Göreme Valley*

*Right: A tree in spring in Rose Valley*

# ASIA

**WHAT IS IT?**
A gorgeous, heavily forested national park, dominated by thousands of sandstone peaks and pillars.

**HOW TO GET THERE:**
Fly to Changsha, then by road to Zhangjiajie.

**WHEN TO GO:**
September to May.

**NEAREST TOWN:**
Zhangjiajie (formerly Dayong) is close to the edge of Wulingyiang.

**DON'T MISS:**
Puguang Temple, the grotto in the Yuhuang Cave.

**YOU SHOULD KNOW:**
Inscribed on the UNESCO World Heritage list in 1992, Wulingyiang was the first area of China to be thus distinguished.

# Wulingyiang Scenic and Historic Interest Area

Located in Hunan Province, Wulingyiang's 26,000-hectare (64,250-acre) site is one of the country's 40 most famous scenic spots, and is inhabited by several tribal groups. Some 3 billion years ago, this was an ancient sea, and today's landscape of eroded quartzite sandstone is the exposed and eroded sea floor. The region contains over 3,000 narrow sandstone pillars and peaks, and of these, over 1,000 rise to over 200 m (656 ft). In amongst them are waterfalls, streams and pools, deep valleys, ravines and complex limestone caves. Almost the entire region is forested – 99 per cent is covered with vegetation, including many rare species.

Zhangjiajie National Forest is covered with primitive, sub-tropical forest. It boasts 191 types of tree, and is absolutely draped in flowers   orchids, azaleas and Giant Mountain lotus scent the air. The Lobster flower, unique to the park, can change colour up to five times a day. Suoxiyu is the largest area of the Park, with a creek running from east to west. The valley floor, made of yellow-green and dark green shale, contrasts with the upper slopes of dark red

*The Tianzi Mountain reserve*

*A Rhesus macaque with her young in Wulingyiang National Park*

or grey quartzite and shale. Huanglong, or Yellow Dragon Cave, is thought to be one of the largest in China. On four levels, it contains an underground lake, two rivers, three waterfalls, 13 halls and 96 corridors.

The Tianzi Mountain reserve is at a much higher elevation and is rich with strangely shaped peaks and rocks. Famously covered in mist and fog, it is renowned for its beautiful views. There are two spectacular natural bridges here – Tianxia Diyi Qiao, or Bridge across the Sky is 40 m (132 ft) long, 10 m (33 ft) wide and 15 m (50 ft) thick. At 357 m (1,171 ft) above the valley, it may be the world's highest natural bridge.

*Following pages: Sandstone pillars shrouded in mist*

# Mount Wuyi

**WHAT IS IT?**
A fabulous landscape of
outstanding biodiversity
and great archaeological
significance
**HOW TO GET THERE:**
By air from many major
Chinese cities, or by train
from Fuzhou
or Xiamen.
**WHEN TO GO:**
October to March
**NEAREST TOWN:**
Wuyishan City 5 km (3 mi)
**DON'T MISS:**
The Ancient Xiamei Folk
Buildings, where tea
merchants, officials and
Confucian scholars built
impressive houses during
the Ming and
Qing Dynasties.
**YOU SHOULD KNOW:**
The Mount Wuyi Scenic
Area is classic tea growing
country, the origin of
Lapsang Souchong and the
famous Da Hong Pao.

Mount Wuyi, in Fujian Province, is the most important
area for biodiversity conservation, riverine beauty and
archaeological significance in south-east China. The
landscape has been formed by volcanic activity, and
eroded by water, and the Nine Bend River, running
clear and deep, makes its way through a deep,
dramatic gorge flanked by sheer, smooth, rock cliffs.

Within this landscape of hills and gorges are a considerable number of ancient temples and monasteries, and although many of them are now completely ruined, the landscape is so perfect one could be looking at a classical Chinese painting.

Mount Wuyi has been protected for 12 centuries, and is the cradle of Neo-Confucianism, a doctrine that was influential in the Far East for hundreds of years. In the 1st century BC, the rulers of the Han dynasty

*Floating down Nine Bend River (Jiugu Xi) on bamboo rafts near Heavenly Tour Peak (Tianyou Feng)*

built a large, walled city at nearby Chengcun, and this, as well as many other sites here, is of great archaeological significance.

This is one of the most outstanding sub-tropical forests in the world. The vegetation is divided into 11 categories, the most common being evergreen broad-leafed forest, and there is a wide diversity of fauna too, including endangered species such as the South Chinese tiger, Clouded leopard and Mainland serow. There are three species here endemic to these mountains, including the Bamboo snake – indeed, this is definitely snake country, 73 species of reptile can be found, and preserved snakes can commonly be seen as part of the decor of local restaurants and pharmacies.

This is an area of almost otherworldly beauty. Drift through the Wuyi Canyon on a raft, gaze at fold upon fold of lush green mountains. Sit peacefully drinking a seriously delicious cup of tea and meditate upon the marvellous nature of our planet.

*A stump-tailed macaque*

# Sunderbans Royal Bengal Tiger Reserve

A World Heritage Site, the Sunderbans Reserve forms the core 2,585 sq km (1,616 sq mi) of the vast Ganges Delta in West Bengal. Here the silt deposits of a continent form islands connected to the mainland by a series of labyrinthine waterways choked with tangled mangroves. Half the world's species and 80% of all India's mangrove swamps make these the most fecund marshes on the planet, able to support the biggest concentration of tigers along with colonies of rhesus macaques, chitals, boar, otters, salt water crocodiles, monitor lizards, king crabs, Ridley's, green and hawk's bill turtles, innumerable snakes and flocks of the most

**WHAT IS IT?**
A World Heritage Site and Biosphere Reserve.
**HOW TO GET THERE:**
By boat and rickshaw from Canning.
**WHEN TO GO:**
September to March
**NEAREST TOWN:**
Gosaba 50 km (31 mi)
**DON'T MISS:**
The cruise down many of the creeks.
**YOU SHOULD KNOW:**
The journey provides the rites of passage to rural Bengal.

*Eye of the Bengal Tiger*

multi-coloured birds on earth or water.

Twice a day, the mangroves flood with the tide, making access especially difficult. The Sunderbans tigers have long adapted to this amphibious habitat. They are adept swimmers, can survive in and on brackish water, and are known to feed on fish and turtles as well as their usual prey. Their proliferation is a measure of the Reserve's success in limiting poaching and human activities like fishing and the collection of wood and forest produce. It also has its downside: Royal Bengal Tigers are notorious man-eaters, accustomed through generations of proximity to the delights of a human snack treat. The use of

electric deterrents, lighting and awareness programmes for villagers and visitors alike has reduced local fatalities from 40 to roughly ten a year. But any risk seems worth the chance of seeing that glorious black-striped, golden-orange flash between the dense greenery.

Reaching the Sunderbans is an adventure. From the nearest rail station at Canning you must find a way to reach Sonakhali, where you take a 7-hour boat ride to Gosaba, followed by a rickshaw to Pakhirala, and another boat to the Park entrance at Sajnekhali. Your reward is seeing the biggest cat on earth in its swampy paradise.

*Sunrise in Sunderbans National Park*

# Kaziranga National Park

**WHAT IS IT?**
A National Wildlife Park and World Heritage Site.

**HOW TO GET THERE:**
By plane to Jorhat, then by road.

**WHEN TO GO:**
November to April

**NEAREST TOWN:**
Jorhat 95 km (59 mi)

**DON'T MISS:**
The early morning.

**YOU SHOULD KNOW:**
You can ride elephants (with mahouts) through the park.

*An Indian One-horned Rhino*

On the banks of the Brahmaputra River in the extreme north-east of India in Assam, the 430 sq km (269 sq mi) of the Kaziranga National Park, a maze of forests, swamps and tall thickets of elephant grass, provide the ideal habitat for the Indian One-horned Rhino. There are more here than anywhere else, along with a large population of Indian elephants, Barasingha and hog deer, sloth bears, tigers, leopards, capped langurs, Hoolock gibbons, wild boar, jackal, buffalo, pythons and jungle otters. It is a breathtaking vision of the teeming potential of successful wilderness parks.

In winter, huge numbers of migratory birds descend on the lakes and marshes. Greylag geese, red-crested pochard, gadwall and northern shoveller are among those splashing down to join the oriental honey buzzard, brahminy kite, white-tailed and Pallas's fishing eagles, Himalayan griffon, and more than 100 other species already resident.

The relatively open country makes watching the wildlife easy. You can usually see all the major species within a single day. Early morning is best, when elephants resume their foraging; and the grasslands are a magnet for circling raptors like the serpent eagle, searching for prey among the flashy kaleidoscope of storks, herons, pelicans and teal for whom the marshes are home.

The park changes with the seasons – the major wildlife migrates to different areas within the park during the monsoon, for example, when the Brahmaputra overflows its banks. It is prudent to check in advance which areas are accessible, and whether permits may be necessary.

*Sunset in Kaziranga National Park*

*Following pages: Indian elephants*

# Sinharaja Forest Reserve

**WHAT IS IT?**
A small area of primary tropical rainforest.
**HOW TO GET THERE:**
By air to Colombo, then by road.
**WHEN TO GO:**
January–April and August-September
**NEAREST TOWN:**
Ratnapura (44 km, 27 mi)
**YOU SHOULD KNOW:**
Leeches can be a problem.

*Sri Lanka blue magpie*

One of the jewels of Sri Lanka, the Sinharaja Forest Reserve lies in the southwest of the island and is its last remnant of pristine tropical rainforest. It is 21 km (13 mi) wide and some 5 km (3 mi) long, and provides a last home for such rare animals as wild boar, barking deer, giant squirrels, civets, porcupines, mongoose , purple-faced langurs and extremely elusive leopards. This area is precious because it holds so many species of plants that no longer occur anywhere else in the world as the forests around them have been cut down. Sinharaja has been declared a UNESCO World Heritage Site because of the importance and rarity of its plants.

There are two main habitats within the reserve – tropical lowland rainforest and tropical wet evergreen forest – and more than half of the major plant species here are found nowhere else.

*Sinharaja rainforest*

The dense forests are home to many species of birds, among them Sri Lanka blue magpie, greater racket-tailed drongo, white-headed starling, orange-billed babbler, red-faced malkoha and the extremely rare green-billed coucal. Among the other creatures that enjoy the lush green wilderness are hump-nosed and green pit vipers and many amphibians, including tree frogs. There is also a wide variety of insect life, including the common birdwing butterfly, another species that occurs only here.

# Sacred Valleys Trek

By anybody's reckoning Bhutan is a most
extraordinary country. Tucked away in the folds of
the eastern Himalayas, and surrounded by China and
India, this remote, mountain kingdom is the last place
in the Himalayas where Mahayana Buddhist culture
survives intact, informing every aspect of life here.
First opened to the world in 1974, the present king's
policy has been tailored to keep Bhutan's traditional

culture and pristine environment untouched by outside influences and so far, so good.

Bumthang is a complex of four beautiful valleys, lying at about 2,600 m (8,500 ft). Buckwheat, barley, potatoes and apples grow in profusion, and this tranquil landscape is Bhutan's sacred heart, containing many of its most revered temples. Trek alongside the Chamkhar River, famed for its trout, visit Thamshing Lhakang Temple, built in the 7th century, and Membar Tsho (Burning Lake) where Guru Rimpoche, who brought Buddhism here from Tibet, hid some sacred scriptures.

Walk through traditional villages of unique architecture, meet delightful local people, marvel at gorgeous handicrafts, climb up to Phephela Pass through serene forests of miniature bamboo, rhododendrons and pine. Follow the course of the river up to the base camp of Gangkhar Puensum. Bhutan's highest mountain at 7,570 m (24,000 ft) is the world's highest, unclimbed mountain. Various attempts to climb it have failed, and mountaineering has been forbidden since 2003 because of local religious beliefs.

Flora and fauna flourish in this environment of respect for all living things, and over 600 bird species can be found, including ten that are endangered. There are 165 different mammals including red panda, Himalayan black bear and tiger. Takin, the national animal, can be seen grazing in alpine meadows, also home to some of the country's remarkable flora. What with temples and fortresses, natural beauty and charming people, trekking Bhutan's Sacred Valleys is a magical experience.

**WHAT IS IT?**
A complex of four high valleys.

**HOW TO GET THERE:**
Fly to Paro. Drive to Thimpu and on to Trongsa and Bumthang.

**WHEN TO GO:**
March - June, and September - November

**NEAREST TOWN:**
Jakar

**DON'T MISS:**
The colourful festivals that take place in the valleys during spring and autumn.
Thanbi Temple, founded in 1470.
Thimpu, Bhutan's capital city.

**YOU SHOULD KNOW:**
Bhutan, (known by its people as 'the Land of the Thunder Dragon') accords great respect to the mountain Gangkhar Puensum. According to folklore it is the source of three major Bhutanese rivers, the Kuru, Chamkhar and Mangde. When they first appeared, the rivers proposed a race, but Chamkhar said she would rather take her time and enjoy the views. This is why the Trongsa and Lhuntse valleys are narrow and steep, while Bumthang valley is wide and lush.

*Taktsang Monastery*

**WHAT IS IT?**
A richly forested mountain range, covering the length of western Sumatra.
**HOW TO GET THERE:**
Plane or ferry to Medan, or plane to Padang, then by road.
**WHEN TO GO:**
May to September, north of the Equator, March to August, south of the Equator.
**NEAREST TOWN:**
Towns and villages are scattered throughout the mountains and up and down the coast.
**DON'T MISS:**
Lake Toba, Bukittinggi.
**YOU SHOULD KNOW:**
The tsunami of 2004 damaged the north-west coast of Sumatra, as did the earthquake of 2007.

# Bukit Barisan Mountains, Sumatra

The Bukit Barisan are a range of mountains running almost the entire length of Sumatra's western side, from Aceh in the north to Lampung in the south, forming the spine of this huge island. It comprises three National Parks, collectively known as the Tropical Rainforest Heritage of Sumatra, and was listed by UNESCO in 2004.

Some 70 million years ago, when tectonic plate collision raised the Himalayas, the Barisan Mountains were also forced upwards along the west coast of the island. Here the mountains often meet the shoreline, while east of the range lie low hills, plains and swamps. The terrain consists mainly of densely forested volcanoes, many of which are still active, and includes, at 3,800 m (12,540 ft), the highest volcanic

peak in Indonesia, Mt. Kerinci. This fabulous mountain range is rich in habitat. Several large rivers rise here and many streams; there are extraordinary lakes such as Lake Toba, Kelimutu Crater Lake and Lake Gunung Tujuh, the highest in South-East Asia, stunning waterfalls, hot springs, smoke-belching fumeroles and complex cave systems.

Above all, Bukit Barisan protects over 10,000 plant species, more than 200 mammals, 22 of which are Asian and not found elsewhere in Indonesia and 15 of which are found solely in Indonesia. Here too are almost 600 bird species, including 21 that are endemic. This is home to orangutans and Asian elephants and is almost the last refuge of the critically endangered Sumatran tiger and Sumatran rhino.

Illegal logging, forest clearance for agriculture and poaching are the main threats to wildlife here – over 6.5 million hectares (16 million acres) of forest have been lost during the last few years. Habitat loss equals loss of prey for larger mammals, and loss of vegetation for herbivores such as rhinos. UNESCO's protection is essential to conserve Bukit Barisan for future generations.

*Equatorial rainforest in the Bukit Barisan Mountains*

*Left: Kelimutu Crater Lake*

# Komodo National Park

Komodo National Park was established in 1980 to protect the ancient monitor lizards of the same name, and was inscribed on the World Heritage List in 1991. The three islands are surrounded by one of the world's best marine environments, with coral reefs, seamounts, seagrass beds and mangroves that harbour more than 1,000 species of fish, 70 species of sponges and 14 species of whales, as well as dolphins, sharks, manta rays, dugong and sea turtles. There are at least 260 species of coral in the reefs. The islands are becoming increasingly popular dive sites.

However, it is the dragons that are the lure for most visitors to these barren volcanic islands in Indonesia's Lesser Sundas. Guided tours take tourists to hot spots when the lizards are active during the morning or late afternoon. During the heat of the middle of the day, they burrow in the dry stream bed to keep cool.

These prehistoric predators can grow up

to 3 m (10 ft) in length. Despite their stumpy-looking legs they can run as fast as a dog and, given the opportunity, could eat a human-being so when on the beautiful beaches in the sandy bays visitors are advised to keep an eye out for their foot- and tail-prints in the sand. They can also swim and have been spotted swimming from island to island.

*Following pages: Damselfish swimming amongst Staghorn Coral.*

*A Komodo Dragon, the world's largest lizard, strolling on a beach looking for food on Komodo Island.*

# The Heart of Borneo

**WHAT IS IT?**
The centre of South East Asia's biodiversity and the world's third largest rainforest.
**HOW TO GET THERE:**
The area is huge so you have a choice of visiting Kalimantan, Sabah, Brunei Darussalam or Sarawak.
**WHEN TO GO:**
Go from March to October to avoid the monsoon.
**NEAREST TOWN:**
Bintulu is an ideal jumping off point for visiting the Sarawak side of the interior, or Kota Kinabalu in Sabah, Tanjung Selor in Kalimantan and Temburong in Brunei.
**DON'T MISS:**
Trek the dense jungle of the Bario Loop to experience authentic Borneo.
**YOU SHOULD KNOW:**
Expect leeches and heavy rain whenever you go.

Home to six per cent of the world's biodiversity, the Heart of Borneo is 220,000 sq km (85,000 sq mi) of largely unspoilt equatorial rainforest spanning the highlands and foothills of Brunei, Sarawak and Sabah. The diverse land is made up of lush jungle, mangroves, mountains, rapid flowing rivers, swamps and limestone peaks and is an area of immense beauty and uncharted territory.

This is one of only two places in the world where rhinos, elephants and orangutans co-exist, and new species are being found at a rate of three every month – 360 new species have been discovered in the last ten years. It is believed the rainforest still harbours new species and a plethora of plants which could hold the key to curing diseases such as cancer and AIDS. Discovering these botanical secrets is a difficult task as the interior is dense, largely inaccessible, jungle. Several other species are currently under threat, including sun bears, clouded

leopards and Bornean gibbons, endemic in the area. This unparalleled biodiversity is now protected under the Heart of Borneo Declaration in recognition of the importance of a forest large enough to sustain successful populations of rare species.

The three governments of the Heart of Borneo – Brunei, Indonesia and Malaysia – have pledged to conserve the rainforest and introduce a network of protected areas. In February 2007 the Heart of Borneo Declaration was signed by all three and they will sustainably manage the area to protect indigenous species and prevent the logging that has been destroying vital habitats. It is hoped that this will protect the 222 species of mammals, 420 bird species, 100 species of amphibians, 394 species of fish and 15,000 plant species in the area. A third of all plants here cannot be found anywhere else.

Indigenous tribes encompassing over thirty ethnic groups still live in the area, sustained by fourteen of Borneo's twenty rivers that flow through this vast space. Living from the land and nurturing ancient traditions these diverse cultures, ranging from Iban and Kayan to Dayak, need the protection of the rainforest to ensure their survival and preservation of a unique way of life.

*Orangutans are highly endangered in the wild and can only be found in the rainforests of Borneo and Sumatra.*

*Left: Sunrise over misty lowland rainforest, Borneo*

**269**

# Camiguin Island

**WHAT IS IT?**
A volcanic island

**HOW TO GET THERE:**
Limited trips available from Cebu by air and sea. Or fly to Cagayan de Oro City, take a bus to Balingoan and boat to the island.

**WHEN TO GO:**
Any time of year (the island is rarely visited by typhoons). April to June is the prime period, November to January the coolest.

**NEAREST TOWN:**
There are five small towns on the island. The capital is Mambajao.

**DON'T MISS:**
Binangawan Falls in Sagay – an unspoiled series of cascades into a single pool.
The Sunken Cemetery (scuba gear required) – immersed beneath the sea after the volcanic eruption of 1871, marked by a large cross.
Tangun Hot Spring at Naasag – an unusual natural seashore pool that is hot at low tide, changing to cool as the tide comes in.

**YOU SHOULD KNOW:**
If this is for you, be careful when you book – there is another Camiguin Island in the Philippines, part of the Babuyan Islands north of Luzon.

The independently minded Camiguin islanders have always fought their corner – unsuccessfully. The Spanish established a settlement in the early 1600s, the Americans invaded in 1901 and proved that bullets were better than *bolos* and spears and the Japanese ruthlessly crushed guerrilla activities in World War II. There was, however, a happy ending in 1946 when the Philippines gained independence.

The pear-shaped island is not large – 230 sq km (90 sq mi) – and is evidently of volcanic origin, as its nickname 'The Island Born of Fire' confirms. There are several large peaks, plus numerous domes and cones. Mount Hibok-Hibok, the largest, is still active, last erupting in 1953. It has hot springs, crater lakes and Taguines Lagoon, a volcanic maar. Hibok-Hibok is a popular destination for hikers, though a permit is required.

This is an island of contrasts, with traditional coastal villages, coconut plantations, lush forests, hot and cold springs, waterfalls, dramatic volcanic landscapes, abundant marine life and pristine beaches. Indeed, Camiguin has one of the world's finest beaches, as voted for by travel journalists – White Island Beach, a bleached sandbar in the turquoise Bohol Sea reached by boat, with great views of Mounts Vulcan and Hibok-Hibok.

Despite national efforts to encourage only sustainable eco-tourism, Camiguin's experience suggests this isn't easy. The newly discovered Camiguin hanging parrot, a handsome green, blue and red bird endemic to this island only, is already under threat as its habitat is eroded by increased economic activity and visitor-friendly development. And the rural tranquility and slow pace of life that makes this enchanted island so appealing is hardly helped by its designation as one of the 'Top 25 Tourist Destinations' in the Philippines.

*Mount Hibok-Hibok*

# Ang Thong Archipelago

Bathed in the aquamarine waters of the Gulf of Thailand about 30 km (20 mi) from Ko Samui, the Ang Thong Archipelago is a collection of 42 uninhabited islands famed for their natural beauty. The islands have been designated a National Marine Park to save them from development and excessive tourism, making them a pleasant and relaxing place to visit. The best way to explore is by boat as most of the islands are close together. Each island is different, but they are characterized by limestone cliffs, tropical forest, caves and secret lagoons, pristine white sand beaches, coral reefs and aquamarine waters.

Ko Mae Ko (Mother Island) is a must-see. Encircled on all sides by limestone cliffs, the emerald lake in the middle of the island is linked to the sea by an underground tunnel. It's a strenuous climb to view the lake but well worth the effort as you gaze down on the stunningly beautiful water and are rewarded by a spectacular view across the whole park.

Other popular islands are Ko Sam Sao (Tripod Island) with its extensive coral reef and Wua Talap

**WHAT IS IT?**
Forty-two beautiful uninhabited islands.
**HOW TO GET THERE:**
Boat from Ko Samui
**WHEN TO GO:**
December to February, August and September

Island (Sleeping Cow Island), the summit of which offers magnificent views across the entire archipelago and the mainland. The headquarters of the national park are situated here, and there is bungalow-style accommodation for visitors. There are caves in many of the islands with intriguing rock formations to discover. The lovely white sandy beaches, many of them deserted, are surrounded by coral reefs and the warm shallow waters are ideal for swimming. Other popular island activities include sea-kayaking and snorkelling around the coral reefs.

*Left: A pristine white sand beach in the Ang Thong National Marine Park*

*A view across the Ang Thong Archipelago*

**NEAREST TOWN:**
Nathon for the ferry
**DON'T MISS:**
Ko Pha-Ngan and Ko Tao are two of the most beautiful islands. Take a sea-kayaking trip or snorkel around the coral reefs.
The salt water lake on Ko Mae Ko – its well worth the walk up to view the lake.
The views from the top of Wua Talap Island.
**YOU SHOULD KNOW:**
Access to the National Park is controlled. Several boat rental companies in Ko Samui are licensed to visit the islands.

# Coral Reefs including the Eye of the Maldives

*Following pages:
Shoaling fusiliers in the
Maldives*

*Far right: An Emperor
Angelfish in the North
Ari Atoll*

*Male Atoll in the
Maldives*

The Maldive Islands are located 480 km (300 mi) south west of Cape Cormorin, on the southern tip of India. Consisting of 26 large atolls containing 1,190 islands, they run 648 km (405 mi) from north to south, and 130 km (81 mi) east to west, a double chain lying within the central area. Only 200 of the islands are inhabited and, of these, some 88 are exclusive holiday resorts.

The geomorphology of the Maldivian islands is unusual. An atoll is a coral formation surrounding a circular lagoon, but these lagoons, many of which are very large, are dotted with other, smaller, ring-shaped reefs, each surrounding its own sandy lagoon. These are known locally as 'faros', and this formation is known as the Eye of the Maldives. Natural channels, allowing the free movement of fish and currents between the lagoons and the open sea, cut through each reef.

The islands are formed from coral sand, and are very low lying, averaging no more than 2 m (6 ft 6 in), with vegetation mainly consisting of coconut palms, and mangroves. Just take a look, however, beneath the surface of the turquoise sea and you will find glorious, dazzling coral gardens teeming with multi-coloured fish that are more curious than afraid of humans. The diving and snorkelling here is the main attraction, and the exclusivity of many of its resorts, which appeals to the rich and famous.

Long term, the Maldives are under threat. Climate change is already adversely affecting the coral, which can only thrive at temperatures from 24 to 27 °C (75 to 81 °F), and the natural phenomena of El Niño and La Niña has caused severe bleaching to some of the formations. Sea levels are also rising, and although preventative work is being done, it seems that these fairy tale coral islands will surely slip beneath the surface of the sea in the not too distant future.

# AUSTRALASIA & OCEANIA

# The Twelve Apostles

Just off the coast of southern Victoria is a spectacular group of limestone sea-stacks. Originally they were known as the sow and her pigs, but were renamed in the 1950s. The howling winds and high seas of the Southern Ocean are eating away at the soft limestone walls of the coast here and these stacks are the remnants of land that has already fallen into the sea. They are under threat themselves: in the winter of 2005, one of them collapsed into the sea in a matter of seconds. The cliffs here are up to 70 m (230 ft) high and the tallest of the apostles is about 45 m (150 ft).

They are a spectacular sight from the clifftops, with the waves crashing against them. The wider area of the Twelve Apostles Marine National Park also has areas where visitors can swim, surf, kayak, snorkel or dive, if weather and wave conditions allow. Diving is permitted both on the wreck of the *Lorc Ard* and in the area of the underwater canyons known as the The Arches, where there are spectacular landscapes of seaweed-covered walls with sea fans, lace corals and sea-mosses. Sometimes there are fur seals playing here, zipping through tunnels and underneath arches.

This is rightly one of the three most popular natural attractions in Australia.

*The spectacular Twelve Apostles at sunset*

# The Wet Tropics of Queensland

In the 1980s, a battle was waged between environmentalists and the federal government on one hand and the timber industry and the state government on the other. This resulted in the addition to the World Heritage List of a 450-km (280-mile) long swathe of the coastal area of northern Queensland between Townsville and Cooktown in order to prevent any more logging in the area. What remains is a unique environment, with plants that are examples of types found on the ancient supercontinent of Gondwana. But the area is not just important as a living relic of evolution, it is also beautiful, with rugged peaks, beautiful sandy beaches, dramatic gorges, dense rainforest and Australia's

**WHAT IS IT?**
A vast area of tropical habitat and a UNESCO World Heritage Site.
**HOW TO GET THERE:**
By air to Cairns, then by road
**WHEN TO GO:**
Any time except December to March when it is hot and humid and the roads are often impassable.
**NEAREST TOWN:**
Cairns

*Left:Wallaman Falls*

*Fan Palms in Daintree Rainforest*

283

**DON'T MISS:**
A swim in a pool in Mossman Gorge.
**YOU SHOULD KNOW:**
Mosquito-repellent is a must at all times in the wet tropics; box jellyfish are a hazard in the sea in the very hot months; before swimming in any river, check with the locals that it is crocodile free.

*Newell Beach*

tallest single-drop falls, the Wallaman Falls, near Trebonne.

Lying between the coast and the Atherton Tablelands and their dry eucalypt habitat, the forests contain eucalypts, banksias and paperbark trees, around the rivers there are swamps, and mangroves protect the coasts. Mossman Gorge, near the town of the same name, has spectacular scenery and lovely swimming holes.

This protected, pristine area, is brimming with wildlife, from cassowaries to tree-kangaroos and golden bowerbirds to yellow-bellied gliders and estuarine crocodiles. Its four national parks are havens for the animals that live in this tiny relic of a habitat that once occupied much of Australia.

# Fraser Island

Stretching 123 km (76 mi) alongside Queensland's coast, Fraser Island is one of the most beautiful places on earth. Made almost entirely of sand, it is unique. Some of the dunes are up to 240 m (790 ft) high. In the lowlands, the heathlands are awash with wildflowers in spring and summer, while in the interior, ancient rainforests surround more than 100 freshwater lakes and grow alongside crystal-clear streams. Among the highlights of the island are the wetlands of the Great Sandy Strait, where dugongs and turtles may be seen, and Hervey Bay during the whale migration season, when more than 1,500 humpbacks pass through. Inland, the lakes are

**WHAT IS IT?**
The largest sand island in the world.
**HOW TO GET THERE:**
By boat from the mainland or by air from Hervey Bay.
**WHEN TO GO:**
Summer, or August–September to watch whales.
**NEAREST TOWN:**
Hervey Bay 15 km (9 mi)
**DON'T MISS:**
Lake Wabby
**YOU SHOULD KNOW:**
Swimming offshore is not recommended because of the rips and sharks.

*Fraser Island is made almost entirely of sand.*

beautiful, particularly Lake Wabby and the lakes round
McKenzie. The northern part of the island has been
designated as a national park. If you drive up the
eastern beach northward from the Pinnacles, you will
pass the 25-km (15-mi) expanse of the Cathedrals –
cliffs made of coloured sand – on your way to Indian
Head, which is a great spot for looking for dolphins,
sharks and whales.

Other wildlife here includes what are probably the

purest strain of dingos (do not feed them: they are
losing their fear of humans and there have been
several fatal attacks), loggerhead turtles, manta rays,
possums, bats, sugar gliders, wallabies, echidnas
and several species of reptile. The most noticeable of
the 200 or so species of bird here are the sulphur-
crested cockatoos, because they make so much
noise, although the rainbow lorikeets are rather
more colourful.

*Following pages:
An aerial view of
Fraser Island*

*Lake McKenzie*

# The Bungle Bungles

**WHAT IS IT?**
A unique mountain range in Western Australia.
**HOW TO GET THERE:**
By road from Halls Creek
**WHEN TO GO:**
April–May, at the beginning of the dry season and before the peak tourist season.
**NEAREST TOWN:**
Halls Creek 190 km (115 mi)
**DON'T MISS:**
Cathedral Gorge and Echidna Chasm.
**YOU SHOULD KNOW:**
A 4 wheel drive is a must as the off-road section of the drive to the park has rough track, steep climbs, tight corners and creeks to cross.

Known to the local Aboriginals as Purnululu, and set in the National Park of the same name, the Bungle Bungles are a unique range of orange, black and white landforms up to 400 m (1,300 ft) high. The sandstone they are made from was laid down about 350 million years ago, and over the last 2 million years, they have been uplifted then eroded into amazing beehive-shaped domes. From the Piccaninny Creek car park, it is a short walk to Cathedral Gorge, a giant natural amphitheatre that carries people's voices round from one side to the other. The full walk through the Piccaninny Gorge requires an overnight camp and some scrambling in places, but is worth it for the stunning views of cliffs, domes, chasms and the sight of Black Rock Pool. In the north of the park, away from the domes, are two gorges: Mini Palms Gorge and Echidna Chasm. The path through the former leads you up 150 m (400 ft) to a platform for

*Sunrise in Purnululu
National Park*

views of the palms in the
valley below, their lush
green contrasting with
the colour of the rocks.
Echidna Chasm is a narrow
gorge with soaring cliffs that
glow in the sunlight, leaving
you almost in the dark at
the bottom.

Even though it takes an
effort to get to this remote
spot, it is worth it: this is a
unique landscape that will
stay in your memory.

*A tourist in Cathedral
Gorge cavern*

291

# Lake Matheson

**WHAT IS IT?**
A glacial lake that provides some of the most stunning views you will ever see.
**HOW TO GET THERE:**
By road, then on foot. The lake is 6 km (4 mi) from Fox Glacier township along Cook Flat Road, and the walk around the lake takes about 70 minutes.
**WHEN TO GO:**
Spring to autumn in good weather.
**NEAREST TOWN:**
Fox Glacier village/Weheka 5 km (3 mi)
**DON'T MISS:**
Sunrise and sunset.

Carved out at the peak of the last ice age some 14,000 years ago by the Fox Glacier, when it was much nearer the Tasman Sea, Lake Matheson provides one of the iconic images of New Zealand, as the peaks of Aoraki/Mount Cook and Mount Tasman are reflected in its still waters, framed by the rainforest that surrounds the lake and protects it from breezes that would disturb its perfect surface. Because the lake bed contains large amounts of dissolved sediment left there by the glacier, its waters are dark, increasing its properties as a mirror.

The forty-minute stroll down to the lake from the

Fox Glacier village leads through beautiful temperate rainforest to the jetty, positioned to give the best possible views. You also catch glimpses of the reflection from the lake-shore path.

If you can, the best times of day to come here are sunrise and sunset. As dawn breaks over the mountains in the east, eerie blue light spills over the snow-covered peaks and down into the valley below, highlighting the mist as the reflection gradually becomes clearer and brighter. At the other end of the day, the mountains take on an orange hue as the sun drops, chased up the mountain sides by ever-deepening shades as it finally drops below the horizon.

*Lake Matheson and the peaks of Mount Tasman and Aoraki*

# Whakarewarewa's thermal valley and mud pools

One of the most active thermal areas in the strange landscape of Rotorua is the Whakarewarewa Thermal Valley, which hosts an eclectic selection of giant mud puddles, fumaroles, steaming hot pools, as well as the geysers of Geyser Flat.

The appearance and behaviour of mud pools depends on the relative proportions of mud and water. In this valley, the mud is quite thick, and the successive bubble-bursts form concentric rings that disappear only very slowly, leaving a landscape of unearthly ridges.

There are roughly 500 pools in the valley, many of

*Whakarewarewa
Thermal Valley*

which are alkaline hot springs. Their edges are encrusted with silica and steam rises over their blue waters, adding to the eeriness of the landscape.

To the local Maori, who have lived here since the early fourteenth century, this area is where the fire goddesses Te Pupu and Te Hoata first came to the surface and the geysers, hot springs and mud pools are caused by their breath.

Locals say that each of the geothermal features here has its own personality and they can tell their moods from how they sound. The land here is continually changing and careful checks are made daily to see whether hot springs are emerging or new cracks are forming. As you walk, swathed in steam, between areas of bubbling mud, and watch water boiling from under the ground, you will probably feel very glad that those checks were made!

*Following pages: Pohutu and Prince of Wales Geysers*

# Stewart Island

**WHAT IS IT?**
An unspoilt wilderness – it is the third largest island in New Zealand.
**HOW TO GET THERE:**
Flights from Invercargill.
**WHEN TO GO:**
The weather can swing dramatically in any given day, but December and January are warmest with temperatures averaging 16.5° C (62 °F).
**NEAREST TOWN:**
Oban is the largest town on Stewart Island.

In Maori legend, if North Island was once the great fish and South Island the canoe, then Stewart Island was its anchor. Due south of Invercargill, the Maori name for the third largest island in New Zealand is Rakiura or Glowing Skies. Gazing at a crimson sun setting over the horizon or the Aurora Australis (Southern Lights) sweeping over inky skies, this is the end of that quest for paradise.

This laidback and unspoilt wilderness reverberates with the sound of birdsong. Parakeets, tui, kaka, bellbirds and robins flutter overhead and sing their hearts out. Eighty-five percent of the island is protected, and it is unadulterated heaven for walkers and birders. Just offshore are albatrosses, blue penguins and petrels. Added to that, the coast is punctuated by endless sandy coves for a swim in the somewhat bracing waters.

*The rugged shores of Stewart Island*

**DON'T MISS:**
Walking the 29 km (18 mi)
Rakiura Track (a circuit out
of Oban) with camping and
huts along the way.
Eating crayfish as fresh as
it gets.
Swim at isolated Mason Bay
– the water may be cold but
kiwis abound.
Ulva Island – tiny island just
offshore and heaving with
wildlife, and plenty of trails.
Paterson Inlet for kayaking
and walking.
**YOU SHOULD KNOW:**
Bring a torch if you are
staying in Oban – there are
no streetlights
at night.

*A Tui on Stewart Island*

Searching for New Zealand's national bird, the kiwi, is at its easiest here. The birds are large and pretty common around the beaches, even during the day. They are so short-sighted and slow they may even bump into bathers.

The only real settlement on the island is Oban. This lazy little fishing village nestles in Halfmoon Bay and has enough shops and cafés to keep the relaxed traveller content. Despite its 7,000 km (4,350 mi) coastline, Stewart Island only has 20 km (12 mi) of roads. Shrug off the cares of the world and relax Stewart-style.

# Manu'a Islands

**WHAT IS IT?**
Three volcanic islands – a
tropical paradise.
**HOW TO GET THERE:**
Via an internal flight from
Pago Pago International
Airport.
**WHEN TO GO:**
Warm and wet (November
to April) or warm and dry
(May to October).
**NEAREST TOWN:**
There are a few small
villages scattered on the
islands.
**DON'T MISS:**
South Ofu Beach, for one of
the most stunning
panoramas of beach, sea
and mountains in the entire
Pacific Ocean.
An adventurous trek to the
huge Judds Crater, a six-
hour hike from Ta'u village.
Some of the world's tallest
sea cliffs on the south
coast of Ta'u.
**YOU SHOULD KNOW:**
Visitors are advised to bring
their own necessities
(including food), as supplies
are not generally on sale in
the Manu'a Islands.

Apart from the 'mainland' of Tutuila, American Samoa extends to Rose Atoll, Swains Island and the Manu'a Islands. The latter group consists of adjacent high volcanic islands – Ta'u, Ofu and Olosega – located 110 km (70 mi) east of Tutuila.

Ta'u is the largest of the three, and the most easterly volcanic island in Samoa. It has American Samoa's high point in Lata Mountain, rising to 966 m (3,170 ft), the group's main airport at Fiti'uta and a boat harbour at Faleasao. A road connects the small villages on the northern shore. The south of the island and its reefs are part of the National Park of American Samoa, which includes the sacred site of Saua – another contender for 'birthplace of the Polynesian people'. Unusually, the park is not owned by the US government, but leased from the islanders. There is no tourist infrastructure, though accommodation can be found in the sleepy villages.

Nearfby Ofu and Olosega are tropical Siamese twins. They are saw-tooth volcanic remains separated only by the narrow Strait of Asaga, and effectively joined by a coral reef. Until recently, it was possible to wade from one island to the other at low tide, but now there is a bridge. Ofu Island has a small airport and boat harbour, together with one village, also Ofu, and a visitor lodge. The National Park extends to this most beautiful of islands, protecting a pristine southern coastline and rainforest. The park is being extended to Olosega, where the small population lives in Olosega village, after a second village (Sili) was destroyed by a hurricane.

There are many places that claim to offer serious travellers the opportunity to discover the 'real' South Pacific, untainted by commercialism – but these islands aren't kidding.

*South Ofu Beach*

**Alamy** Aditya 'Dicky' Singh 254; AfriPics.com 36, 38-9; Barry Mason 272; Bluered/CuboImages 231; Carlotta 270-1; Clearview 198-9; Dave & Sigrun Tollerton 284; David Hosking 259; David Robertson 196-7; David South 296-7; Dieter Ziegler/F1online 154-5; Emil Enchev 207; F1online 159; Francis Tokeley/Robert Harding World Imagery 262; G P Bowater 176-7; Galen Howell/Mountain Light 218, Gavin Hellier 239; H Lansdown 299; Images & Stories 148-9; Jaubert Images 180; Jean du Boisberranger/Hemis 230; John Sylvester 49; John-Patrick Morarescu/Westend61 158; Justine Pickett/Papilio 255; Karl Lehmann/Lonely Planet Images 33; Kevin Schafer 256-7, 258; Last Refuge/Robert Harding World Imagery 188; Louise Murray 219; Maria Grazia Casella 283; Martin Siepmann/Westend61 222-3; Michael Krabs/imagebroker 240-1; Navé Orgad 7 right, 273; niceartphoto 175; Pavel Filatov 2, 212, 213; Peter Adams Photography 150-1; Peter de Clercq 211; Peter Hendrie/Lonely Planet Images 301; Philippe Body/Hemis 145; Photoshot 276-7; Radius Images 282; Reinhard Dirscherl 232, 275; RIA Novosti 215; Stephen Spraggon 186-7; Steve Bloom Images 30; Tom Mackie 173, 181, 183, 200-1; Wildlife 138-9, 201

**Corbis** 165, 285; Alison Wright/National Geographic Society 110-1; Andy Rouse 26; Atlantide Phototravel 163, 233; Barry Brown/Visuals Unlimited 98-9; Bernd Kohlhas 220-1; Blaine Harrington III 242-3, 260; Burden, Russell/Index Stock 60-1; Carl & Ann Purcell 75; Christian Kober/Robert Harding World Imagery 248-9, 292-3; Creasource 146-7; Crista Jeremiason/Zuma Press 62; Danny Lehman 78-9; David Muench 63; Dieter Mendzigall/Sodapix 204-5; DLILLC 108, 109; epa/Alejandro Bolivar 86; Erich Kuchling/Westend61 166; Farrell Grehan 72-3; Fiona Rogers 14-15; Francesc Muntada 225, 226; Franck Guiziou/Hemis 178-9; Frank Lukasseck 136-7; Frank Siteman/Science Faction 185; Frans Lanting 8-9, 12, 13, 25, 29, 119, 120-1, 251, 268, 278-9, 298; Fridmar Damm 236-7; Galen Rowell 116; Gavin Hellier/Robert Harding World Imagery 16-17; George H H Huey 56-7, 66-7; George Steinmetz 20; Gregory Gerault/Nordicphotos 141; Guenter Rossenbach 162; Hans Strand 7 left, 142, 152; Image Source 135, 157, 294-5; Jane Sweeney/JAI 105, 106-7; Joe McDonald 265; Jon Arnold/JAI 172; Karl Kinne 55; Keren Su 83; Kevin Schafer 112, 114; Li Xiaoguo/Xinhua Press 250; Marco Cristofori 235; Marco Simoni/Robert Harding World Imagery 127; Mark Karrass 52; Martin Harvey 6 left, 21, 22-3; Maurizio Lanini 167; Micah Wright/First Light 286-7; Michael & Patricia Fogden 84-5, 88-9; Michael S Yamashita 216-7; Momatiuk–Eastcott 42-3, 133; moodboard/Yevgen Timashov 244; Nick Rains 291; Nigel Hicks/Purestock/SuperStock 182; Nik Wheeler 96-7; Ocean 18-19, 46-7, 100-1, 170-1, 192-3; Pablo Corral Vega 128; Patrick Escudero/Hemis 95; Peter Adams 190; Peter Essick/Aurora Photos 288-9; Radius Images 53, 76, 77, 202-3, 281; Rene Mattes/Hemis 208; Ron Watts 6 right, 50-51; Russ Heinl/All Canada Photos 45; Sakis Papadopoulos/Robert Harding World Imagery 274-5; Sergio Pitamitz/Robert Harding World Imagery 227; Seth Resnick/Science Faction 269; Shubroto Chattopadhyay 69; Specialist Stock 80-1; Staffan Widstrand 115; Stephen Frink 91, 266-7; Stuart Forster/Robert Harding World Imagery 252-3; Theo Allofs 123, 124-5, 130-1, 169, 290-1; Third Eye Images 54; Tim Graham 71; Tim Hauf/Visuals Unlimited 35; Tony Arruza 102-3; W Cody 59; Walter Geiersperger 160-1; Wayne Lawler/Ecoscene 263; Yann Arthus-Bertrand 92-3, 228-9; Yevgen Timashov/Beyond 245, 246-7

**Getty Images** Flickr/An underwater view in Indonesia 10

**Ron Callow** 65, 70, 191, 194

**Polly Manguel** 64

**Thinkstock** iStockphoto 41